What people

The Way ᴏ₁ ₜₕₑ ᵣₐ.....

Rabbits are everywhere and nowhere, often glimpsed but seldom seen for what and who they are. In *The Way of the Rabbit*, Mark Hawthorne gracefully helps us see our small-bodied, big-eared co-voyagers in a new light. If you love rabbits, he will deepen your understanding. If you don't love rabbits—you soon will.
Carl Safina, author of *Becoming Wild: How Animal Cultures Raise Families, Create Beauty, and Achieve Peace*

I was delighted from the first page to the last. From Easter Bunny origin stories to the presence of lagomorphs in literature and the arts, rabbits in popular culture come alive through Mark Hawthorne's gentle and funny prose—and even better, so does the sweetness and intelligence of real rabbits. Rabbits in nature, rabbits in the house, they're all here and exceptionally good company.
Barbara J. King, author of *Animals' Best Friends: Putting Compassion to Work for Animals in the Wild and Captivity*

What a lovely tribute to our furry rabbit friends! Hawthorne's admiration shines through in this thorough telling of the story of Leporidae. It's an enlightening and enchanting account of an animal most of us love but, it turns out, barely know.
Jennifer S. Holland, author of the *Unlikely Friendships* series

By delving into details of the science and sensibilities of rabbits, *The Way of the Rabbit* journeys into the lives and minds of these amazing beings.
Gay Bradshaw, PhD, author of *Elephants on the Edge* and *Talking with Bears*

The Way of the Rabbit is an insightful book that describes who rabbits are and how they have been part of our world for millennia, appearing in various forms of human art and cultural expression. This well-researched volume engenders a deeper appreciation for these gentle creatures and encourages us to treat them with kindness and respect.

Gene Baur, author of *Farm Sanctuary: Changing Hearts and Minds About Animals and Food*

Mark Hawthorne's latest book, *The Way of the Rabbit*, delves deep into the place of rabbits in society and culture. As rabbits have, over the past few decades, gained new status as companion animals and animals deserving of respect and compassion, the scholarship on rabbits is maturing as well. *The Way of the Rabbit* brings new light to the complex narratives that we tell about these animals, and about ourselves as well. *The Way of the Rabbit* is for people who care about rabbits, but also for people who care about animals and our relationships with them.

Margo DeMello, coauthor of *Stories Rabbits Tell: A Natural and Cultural History of a Misunderstood Creature*

Mark Hawthorne shows that each and every individual rabbit is a sentient, feeling being with a unique personality, and every single one deserves to be treated with respect, compassion, and empathy. This wide-ranging book is sure to be a game-changer.

Marc Bekoff, PhD, author of *The Animals' Agenda: Freedom, Compassion, and Coexistence in the Human Age* and *Canine Confidential: Why Dogs Do What They Do*

This very informative and in-depth book about rabbits has some excellent and entertaining chapters on the rabbit in art, literature, myth, and popular culture, which I particularly enjoyed.

Libby Joy, The Beatrix Potter Society

The Way
of the Rabbit

The Way
of the Rabbit

Mark Hawthorne

CHANGEMAKERS
BOOKS

Winchester, UK
Washington, USA

JOHN HUNT PUBLISHING

First published by Changemakers Books, 2021
Changemakers Books is an imprint of John Hunt Publishing Ltd., No. 3 East Street,
Alresford, Hampshire SO24 9EE, UK
office@jhpbooks.com
www.johnhuntpublishing.com
www.changemakers-books.com

For distributor details and how to order please visit the 'Ordering' section on our website.

Text copyright: Mark Hawthorne 2020

The excerpt from "Song of the Rabbits Outside the Tavern" is used by permission of The Marsh
Agency Ltd., on behalf of the Estate of Elizabeth Coatsworth.

ISBN: 978 1 78904 793 6
978 1 78904 794 3 (ebook)
Library of Congress Control Number: 2020949239

A CIP catalogue record for this book is available from the British Library.

Design: Stuart Davies

UK: Printed and bound by CPI Group (UK) Ltd, Croydon, CR0 4YY
Printed in North America by CPI GPS partners

We operate a distinctive and ethical publishing philosophy in
all areas of our business, from our global network of authors to
production and worldwide distribution.

Contents

Because of Cameron, Frankie, Laxmi, Melville, Nibbles, Peri, and Sophie

We who play under the pines,
We who dance in the snow
That shines blue in the light of the moon
Sometimes halt as we go,
Stand with our ears erect,
Our noses testing the air,
To gaze at the golden world
Behind the windows there.
—Elizabeth Coatsworth

Introduction

It would be difficult to identify an animal more universally admired than the rabbit. Maybe it's that rabbits are ubiquitous in nature and yet somewhat mysterious—fully present while remaining mostly concealed. We respect their independence and resourcefulness. To see a rabbit or a hare (who are closely related to rabbits) in the wild, possibly nibbling on vegetation or hopping about with their mates, is to experience a moment of pure joy. For an instant, time stands still. This helps explain why rabbits and hares figure prominently in the mythology, folklore, and religions of so many ancient civilizations, some of which have even credited them with having supernatural powers. Farmers in Britain, for instance, were once so astonished by the colossal number of rabbits in their fields that they believed both the females and males could give birth. Or perhaps it's that rabbits are the subject of countless children's stories and are symbols of innocence, good luck, and abundance. It's little wonder that so many people yearn to share their homes with these lively animals.

Such is the attitude that inspired *The Way of the Rabbit*. I set out to explore, as much as a person can within a humble book, what makes rabbits special. Their friendships, their courage, their history, their playfulness, their spirits, their ability to forgive. This is what I mean by their *way*; rabbits are a physical manifestation of harmony, at once both perfectly at home in the natural world and an elemental part of humanity's spiritual traditions. But I had another motivation for writing this.

As a longtime rabbit lover, I have amassed a modest collection of books relating to the cultural history of rabbits over the years. And while these volumes all add to the wealth of knowledge we have on these long-eared ambassadors of mirth and mischief, each of them includes text or images illustrating in exquisite detail how rabbits are painfully exploited for animal testing, fur, meat, entertainment, and even the pet industry. That is understandable and not a criticism of these titles; people have used rabbits for as long as they believed they could benefit from doing so, and it's important to educate the public about this. Yet as I vainly sought a nonfiction book that did not dwell on how humanity abuses rabbits—one that I could share with fellow sensitive rabbit lovers—it became apparent that I might fill a niche in the lagomorph literature by creating such a title myself. Here, then, you have a book that not only celebrates these charismatic animals but also focuses on the positive aspects of their lives. Only because humans began domesticating rabbits as a source of food will the volume you're holding even superficially allude to them as farmed animals.

You may be surprised to learn, as I was, that during the nineteenth century some commentators believed that rabbits were rather stupid animals incapable of returning the affection of humans. "There are not many stories to be told about the Rabbit, because it is not very clever, and does not do much that we can tell about," wrote one detractor. "It does not appear possible to teach rabbits any kind of tricks," declared another, "and they do not appear even to know their names." An author who claimed to have had 30 years' experience with tame rabbits opined that they were "the most foolish of created beings," adding, "I never saw the remotest glimmer of understanding in any one of them." Writing in a respected natural history tome from 1870, another critic dismissed rabbits as "odd, quaint, and ludicrous beings" who are full of "absurd airs of assumed dignity."

This was in an era when rabbits were gaining wide

popularity as companion animals both in the United Kingdom and the United States, and yet we didn't seem to be making any substantial effort to comprehend them. Characteristic of Victorian children's literature is *Snowdrop: Or the Adventures of a White Rabbit*, a pseudo-autobiography in which the protagonist declares: "As a rule, the world does not allow any large amount of intelligence to individuals of my race, because, ordinarily, we remain motionless, and with eyes fixed." Such is the belief of many people whose only interaction with rabbits is through the wire mesh of a hutch or the bars of a cage. Fortunately, our opinion of rabbits has become more enlightened, and we can see them for the intelligent, loving animals they are.

Yet this has been a slow process, not just with regard to rabbits but animals in general. The question of whether or not animals are sentient — whether they have the capacity to perceive the world, feel sensations, and experience awareness — has long been a subject of debate among scientists. René Descartes, the seventeenth-century scientist, famously believed that animals were merely machines, incapable of either thinking or feeling. Later scientists who believed in animal sentience were (and still are) attacked for their "anthropomorphism." When Donald Griffin, a highly respected zoologist who discovered how bats use sonar to navigate, published his book *The Question of Animal Awareness* in 1976 and suggested that animals engage in meaningful thought processes, his colleagues worried about his mental state. Much had changed two decades later, when the academic journal *Animal Cognition* was founded. It seems that at long last we are beginning to accept that animals such as rabbits lead complex inner lives.

My own fascination and experience with rabbits, which I will elaborate on in due course, began as a cartoon-loving youngster. (What can I say? I was raised amid urban and suburban landscapes, where wild rabbit sightings are about as common as quiet neighbors.) I admired the way Ricochet Rabbit was able to outrun bullets. And I was impressed by Thumper's ability to skate across a frozen pond—*backward*—in Disney's version of *Bambi*. When I discovered books, I had a special fondness for the Peter Rabbit stories and the Rabbit character from *Winnie-the-Pooh*, who was illustrated as a genuine rabbit, not a stuffed animal like Pooh and most of his other friends.

With all these cultural influences, you can probably understand why I was about eight years old before I realized that rabbits did not, in fact, walk upright and speak English. Little did I know as well that you could have a real, live rabbit in your home. After all, none of my friends lived with a rabbit. Dogs, cats, mice, turtles, and lizards, sure, but an actual rabbit wasn't even on my radar, let alone my wish list. My childhood would have likely been much different had our family lived with one or two bunnies. At the very least I would have been the envy of every kid in the neighborhood. But I was probably too immature to fully appreciate rabbits at so young an age—I was an exceptionally clumsy child who could barely be trusted near hardwood furniture, let alone a petite form with a heartbeat—and it is undoubtedly for the best that I did not truly "discover" them as living beings until many years later. By that time, rabbits would have a place in my life that I could hardly have imagined in my youth.

Although this book is filled with information about rabbits, it's not a primer explaining methods for bunny-proofing your home, what to feed them, or which fillers are best for a litter box (pick up a copy of *House Rabbit Handbook: How to Live with an Urban Rabbit* for that). Instead, through the following nine chapters we'll take a sometimes-lighthearted journey and explore the rabbit's role in popular culture, art, history, language, and of course Easter. We will have a peek at their biology and consider their significance as companion animals. And we will examine how rabbits have influenced the mythic traditions of many cultures, including those of Europe, Mesoamerica, and Asia.

Speaking of Asia, it is revealing that in Chinese astrology, the character traits commonly attributed to humans born in the Year of the Rabbit include compassion, sensitivity, modesty, and creativity. These people tend to be quiet homebodies, it is said, and they crave comfort and privacy, free from disturbance and chaos. But they are balanced enough to also appreciate good company and are a kind and helpful friend; indeed, they are skilled at making those around them happy. The rabbit-person is generous to a fault, organized, and never complains. As you will see in the ensuing pages, there could hardly be a more apt description of rabbits themselves. Except maybe the part about never complaining.

Chapter One

Habitat and Conservation

Master Rabbit I saw
In the shadow-rimmed mouth
Of his sandy cavern,
Looking out to the South.
—Walter de la Mare

In April of 1960, a civil engineer named Aubrey Barrett was in southern England directing his crew as they dug a pipe trench across a West Sussex field for the Portsmouth Water Company. Suddenly, amid the soil and rocks their JCB trencher machine was unearthing came some unexpected materials: fragments of pottery. Barrett suspected the pieces were old, but he didn't want to delay the job, so he told his team to keep working. As they dug deeper, the men began exhuming bits of colored tiles. Barrett could now see that he had little choice. He halted the digging and notified local archeologists, who determined the artifacts were from a 2000-year-old mosaic floor. Soon as many as 120 volunteers were busy excavating the largest Roman villa in England. The enormous site, known today as the Fishbourne Roman Palace and Gardens, covers a little more than 5 acres (2 hectares) and took nine painstaking years to uncover.

Among the discoveries at Fishbourne, which include a hundred rooms and a hypocaust system to heat the floors, was a portion of bone just 1.6 inches (4 cm) long. Found in 1964, the unidentified specimen, thought to be from a hare, was placed in a cardboard box and filed away with about 300,000 other excavated pieces. And there it remained, unrecognized, until 2017 when zooarcheologist Fay Worley arrived at the site's archives to examine the bones of brown hares. Upon seeing the small fragment, she knew it wasn't large enough to be from a hare. "I think this might be a rabbit," she told her colleagues.

Genetic analysis proved it was indeed a rabbit tibia, a leg bone that fits between the knee and the ankle. Moreover, radiocarbon dating showed that the tiny tibia came from a rabbit who'd lived around the year 1 CE. With one small bone, Dr. Worley demonstrated that the Romans had introduced rabbits into Britain more than a thousand years earlier than previously thought. And because the bone shows no blade marks, researchers believe it came from a rabbit who was considered a pet rather than food. The national heritage organization Historic England ranked her breakthrough as one of the ten most fascinating archeological discoveries of the decade.

No one is certain who owned the palace, although it was clearly someone with great wealth, possibly a king. What we do know is that the buildings caught fire sometime between 270 and 280 CE and the palace was destroyed. After serving briefly as a burial ground and then farmland—plow marks can still be seen cutting into the intricate mosaic floors—the land eventually returned to its natural state and became a pasture. By the time Aubrey Barrett and his trench digger arrived in 1960, sheep had been grazing above the forgotten ruins for centuries, though bits of tile had found their way to the surface over the years. (The Tudor name for the area, Fittenhalle Field, meaning "Field of the Fallen Hall," hints that fifteenth- and sixteenth-century Britons suspected what lay beneath their feet.) Work continues at the site, with experts like Dr. Worley sifting through and interpreting remains, although we will probably know almost nothing about the rabbit or rabbits who lived there. I like to imagine this particular bunny enjoying a life of some privilege as a pampered companion. Perhaps they were taken into one of the gardens during the day and given a safe place to bunk down at night. How fascinating to think they might have been the first rabbit brought into the country!

The work of researchers like Fay Worley shows how drastically our knowledge of rabbits can be altered. It's also a further demonstration of how valuable rabbits are in our culture and how their individual history can shape our perception of humanity.

Another example that turned our understanding of rabbits on its head is the announcement in 2008 that paleontologists working in India had collected an ankle bone and a heel bone of an ancient rabbit relative who lived some 53 million years ago. "This is thirty-five million years older than anything that's ever been called a lagomorph in India, totally unexpected," said lead researcher Kenneth Rose, a professor in the Center for Functional Anatomy and Evolution at the Johns Hopkins University School of Medicine in Baltimore. Dr. Rose told me that although he believes the bones represent a previously unknown species, "as no other lagomorphs of this age are known from India or anywhere in southern Asia," there are not enough remains to say for certain. Regardless, such developments illustrate why it is impossible to pinpoint precisely how many species of rabbits there are in the world: thanks to research, the numbers continue to be revised, so currently the best we can say is there are 31 known species. And that's just the rabbits; there are also 32 known species of hares and 29 known species of pikas, both of which, along with rabbits, belong in the taxonomic order Lagomorpha.

As Dr. Rose's work suggests, rabbits and hares likely originated in Asia during the Eocene period, which lasted from approximately 55 to about 34 million years ago. They gradually made their way to North America and Europe and eventually expanded into Africa and South America. Today lagomorphs comprise two families: Ochotonidae (pikas) and Leporidae (rabbits and hares). It was some 65 million years ago that the ancestor of all ochotonids and leporids diverged from rodents — right about the time that non-avian dinosaurs went extinct, which paleontologists believe made it possible for mammals such as rabbits, hares, and pikas to diversify and flourish. As with many things evolutionary, however, not all scientists agree on these time periods, with some experts speculating it was closer to 85 million years ago that lagomorphs split from rodents.

Some researchers even believe that rabbits and hares are more closely related to primates than they are to mice and rats. Go back far enough on the evolutionary tree and you will find a superorder of mammals called Euarchontoglires, the living members of which include lagomorphs and humans. It's because of this, says Polina Perelman, a research scientist at Russia's Institute of Molecular and Cellular Biology, that rabbits probably share something like 96 percent of their DNA with humans — that's a little less than the percentage we share with chimpanzees, who are widely considered our closest living relatives. This is just an estimate, Dr. Perelman emphasizes, since genomic sequencing in rabbits has not been as closely studied as in other animals.

The lagomorph species that has certainly been studied the most is the European rabbit, whose Latin name, *Oryctolagus cuniculus*, means "hare-like digger of underground tunnels" because of their fondness for building subterranean homes. They are native to the Iberian Peninsula, the southwestern tip of the European continent that was once part of the Roman Empire. Today the largest country on the peninsula is Spain, which got its name from the Roman word for the nation, Hispania, which was in turn derived from what the Carthaginians called it in 300 BCE, Ispania, meaning "land of the rabbits." From Hispania it's only a short etymological hop to España, which is how the Spanish refer to their country.

The Romans loved the easily domesticated European rabbit and brought them to the farthest points of their realm, where they kept them in walled enclosures called *leporaria*, which were landscaped parks, some quite large and housing pigs and deer as well. (Some biologists speculate that by disseminating *Oryctolagus cuniculus* so widely beyond their initial European range, the Romans may have saved the species from extinction.) Over the centuries sailors from these lands carried them so far that eventually the European rabbit had been introduced onto every continent but Antarctica. Another group responsible for the widespread distribution of rabbits was—believe it or not—lighthouse keepers, often with unfortunate results to local ecologies. In the early years of the twentieth century, for instance, lightkeepers had released a number of rabbits onto the San Juan Islands off the coast of Washington State. By 1924, the digging of the rapidly expanding rabbit population on one island had so undermined the terrain that people could barely walk across the landscape without the ground crumbling beneath them. Eventually, the resident seabirds had to find a more hospitable port to call home.

Introducing a non-native species is nearly always a tricky proposition, and this probably has no better exemplar than Australia, where in 1859 a British colonizer named Thomas Austin had a couple dozen rabbits brought over from England and then released them onto some land near Melbourne. "The introduction of a few rabbits could do little harm and might provide a touch of home," he said. Nature would quickly prove Austin to be disastrously shortsighted. In the absence of natural predators, the 24 rabbits multiplied with such enthusiastic velocity that within a decade the country considered them an agricultural menace—and they still do. A short time later, European rabbits were also released in New Zealand, with similar results.

Geographically, lagomorphs tend to live in temperate zones, which lie between the subtropics and the polar regions and are where the widest seasonal variations occur. This habitat pattern is in contrast to most other species, who tend to live in the middle latitudes near the equator. For more than a hundred years, scientists have debated why the majority of species reside in these midlatitudes, with one theory suggesting it's simply because most animals and plants have been there longer.

Wherever wild rabbits live, two fundamental requirements are key to their survival. First, they need suitable shelter, not only where they can sleep and hide from predators but also where they can keep warm or cool. And second, they need an adequate source of food in close proximity to home. Estimates on how much territory a rabbit will live on their entire life are all over the map, so to speak—some say about 1 acre (0.4 hectares), others say more than 100 acres (40 hectares)—but biologists seem to agree that the smaller the animal, the less acreage they occupy.

Large or small, the landscape of those acres can include desert, meadow, forest, grassland, or wetland, since each rabbit species has unique needs. Cottontail rabbits don't dig burrows and are quite content sheltering beneath shrubs, in tall grass, under fallen trees, or wherever they can conceal themselves. (They might use an unoccupied den or burrow during winter, however.) Rock rabbits inhabit rocky terrain in African deserts. Pygmy rabbits, the smallest known rabbit species in the world, are typically found in areas with dense sagebrush; they construct complex burrows with openings near sagebrush plants, which they eat. Marsh rabbits live by marshes and swamps, feeding on aquatic plants and diving into the water to avoid predators.

European rabbits prefer dry areas with soft soil that they can really sink their paws into, creating extensive burrows with a radius of 50 feet (15 m) or more. To help keep out the rain, rabbits will often burrow into the side of sloping terrain, so the entrance is not facing skyward. Some rabbits favor open land adjacent to covered habitat so they can feed in one and seek cover in the other. They have also adapted to living near humans, and you may observe European rabbits making themselves perfectly at home in city parks, cemeteries, flowerbeds, and other green spaces. My fondest memory from a summer trip my wife and I took to Denver some years ago is returning to our hotel early one evening to find a dozen brown rabbits safely grazing on a narrow strip of lawn between the parking lot and the sidewalk.

Nearly as important as food and shelter to the animals' survival—I suppose some rabbits might argue even *more* important—are other rabbits. Although some species such as the Eastern cottontail are solitary as adults, associating with others only to reproduce, most rabbits are social and live in colonies. Dominant rabbits require submissive acts from all the other rabbits; this typically means a subordinate animal has to retreat or flee from a "leader." In pairs, the female rabbit does most of the digging work for the burrow while the male generally looks on, though he may scrape a shallow hole to demonstrate his dominance to neighboring males and then quickly lose interest. As many as 30 rabbits might occupy a complex series of burrows, known collectively as a warren, and everyone plays a role in a specific hierarchy, with the dominant pair sleeping in the center of the warren.

Just which of the two rabbits within a dominant couple is actually the "leader" is something of a gray area among biologists and others who study lagomorphs. In the wild, most if not all rabbit colonies appear to have a male to whom every other rabbit is subordinate, while among groups of domesticated rabbits, including house rabbits, a matriarchy seems to prevail. What is undeniable is that females do the bulk of the work— not just creating burrows and giving birth but also coming to the defense of their young when necessary, ejecting large cats and even hawks from a nesting site. Moreover, it is always the female who, perhaps dissatisfied with her old home and driven by her rapidly developing pregnancy, initiates a new colony, excavating the burrow and setting up the underground household. She is the stabilizing force in the rabbit community.

Although some pairs may mate for life, rabbits are not

necessarily monogamous. Evidence suggests mating practices are often dictated by warren size, with bonded pairs remaining exclusive in small warrens and rabbits more likely to "play the field" in larger warrens. The physical structure of the warren may also play a part, with isolated burrows providing adequate space for a faithfully bonded couple to occupy, even in large warrens.

Because *Oryctolagus cuniculus* is the only rabbit to have been domesticated, all varieties of tame rabbits today are descendants of this species. There has been much speculation about exactly how and when rabbits came to be domesticated, with one often-cited story claiming that French monks began to tame them as food animals in or about 600 CE. This was accepted as fact by many scientists, including archeologist and evolutionary biologist Greger Larson, who studies animal domestication at the University of Oxford. Among his research, Dr. Larson has examined how gray wolves gradually evolved—the jaws becoming smaller, the ears flopping, the paws shrinking, the disposition growing docile—into the dogs we know today, a process that began more than 15,000 years ago.

In 2015, Dr. Larson turned his attention to how rabbits went from feral to friendly, and he and his team were shocked to discover that the entire story of the monks raising rabbits was apocryphal and based on the simplest of blunders: someone had confused the name of one historical figure with that of another. It seems that in 1936, a German geneticist named Hans Nachtsheim claimed that in 600 CE, Pope Gregory the Great decreed it acceptable to eat rabbits during Lent, supposedly prompting Catholic monks to begin breeding them. Trouble is, that bit of rabbit history is linked not to Pope Gregory but to a religious chronicler named Saint Gregory of Tours—who would no doubt be the first to point out that he was not only an entirely different person but was actually relating a story of someone who became ill *and died* after eating a rabbit. The error of Herr Nachtsheim eventually led to an origin myth that has persisted for years.

"It all made sense," Dr. Larson told me. "It was all very intuitive. We realize now that the story of it being wrong is kind of fun, but the real story for me is why did we buy the story so quickly? Why had nobody really questioned this? That led to this lazy citation and slight embellishment of the story to fit our preconceived notions of domestication, which I now realize are about as wrong as they could possibly be." This is not to suggest that the history of rabbit domestication doesn't have any connection at all to monasteries or other religious institutions. Some of the earliest archeological records of rabbits in central and northern Europe have, in fact, been excavated from monastic ruins, including those from an eleventh- or twelfth-century site at La Charité-sur-Loire in France and from the twelfth- or thirteenth-century Belgian sites Ename Abbey and Dune Abbey.

While researchers are apt to say that what they study is the most important subject for better understanding the world, Dr. Larson believes the strongest argument could be made for the study of domestication, since there isn't any major global problem that does not find its origin there:

> That's everything from climate change to global populations to inequality within society. All this stuff is a direct result of people and animals and plants, for that matter, getting in much closer relationships that build this whole cycle of the emergence of settled agriculture and then domestication, which then allows for a whole suite of other developments, including much larger population sizes and the stratification of society and having free time. Then you start engineering the landscape in a way to take care of that, so now you have ecosystem management and ecosystem degradation, and it just spins out of control from there.

Dr. Larson and his colleagues do not offer an alternative explanation or timeline for rabbit domestication, although they note that our relationship with rabbits as companions could have begun in earnest in the eighteenth century, because that's when we can see the skeletons of tame rabbits start to look different from the skeletons of wild ones. Beyond that, however, we understand very little. What we do know, he says, is that more than many other species, rabbits occupy just about every conceivable way in which humans perceive an animal. "There's the in-home pet, which in the context of all animal domestication is the rarest circumstance for animals to be in." He notes that rabbits are also used in medical research. "And they feature in films and pop culture and major religious festivals, like Easter, in a way that many other animals don't." Even though rabbits have only come into close proximity and established relationships with people over the last 2000 years, he adds, "they now occupy our mental landscape in a way that supersedes a lot of the domestic animals that have a much longer history with us."

Part of that mental landscape has become focused on some rapidly declining rabbit populations. The Annamite striped rabbit, for instance, a species discovered in Vietnam in 1999, is already listed as endangered due to deforestation and hunting. Climate change has left the riverine rabbit of South Africa perilously vulnerable. Amami rabbits, designated as a national treasure in Japan where they live on just two islands, suffered from predation by invasive mongooses. After severe flooding along the San Joaquin River in central California in 1997, biologists believed the riparian brush rabbit had completely disappeared; they were delighted when some members of the species reappeared a decade later, though their numbers are still quite low. In Spain, Portugal, and France, even the European rabbit is in danger of extinction from disease and hunting. Indeed, of the 63 known species of rabbits and hares, 22 are considered near threatened to critically endangered.

The good news is that in many places, conservation programs are making a big difference. One such location is the Columbia Basin of Washington State, where a population of grapefruit-sized pygmy rabbits has long been geographically separated from the rest of their species and has become the subject of valiant efforts to restore their dwindling numbers — in 2001, it was estimated there were fewer than 50 individuals remaining. After some failed attempts at captive breeding and reintroducing, biologists changed their strategy and built an outdoor, fenced enclosure resembling a natural habitat where pygmy rabbits could thrive and reproduce in safety. Since 2011, some 2000 rabbits have been successfully released in the Columbia Basin, although a wildfire in 2020 was a huge setback.

For years, Mexico's volcano rabbit has been under threat from logging, urban development, grass harvesting, and animal agriculture (though not, as it happens, volcanoes). This tiny, short-eared lagomorph lives just outside Mexico City and became the subject of energetic discussion in 2018 when several news outlets suggested that the volcano rabbit, also known as *teporingo* or *zacatuche*, had become extinct. These reports turned out to be wrong, but they highlighted how vulnerable the animals are. Biologist Yajaira García Feria believes that although volcano rabbits have been given government protection, Mexico's residents play a vital role in ensuring the species' survival. "Local people have great power over the conservation (or not) of the forests with the activities that they carry out day by day," she wrote in 2019. These activities include not only monitoring volcano rabbit populations but also raising awareness about the environment within communities.

Loss of habitat has also hurt New England cottontails, whose numbers have dwindled in recent decades and are currently restricted to southern Maine, southern New Hampshire, and parts of Connecticut, Massachusetts, Rhode Island, and New

York east of the Hudson River—in all about one-fifth of their historic range. One solution to restoring their numbers has been to install an initial group of 13 cottontails from Cape Cod onto Nomans Land Island, a 628-acre (254-hectare) national wildlife refuge about 3 miles (5 km) off the coast of Martha's Vineyard. Officials from the US Fish and Wildlife Service say the remote island can support about 600 cottontails, though their goal is that the five females and eight males will eventually become a population of about 500. Then, if all goes well, biologists can begin transplanting some rabbits back into appropriate habitats on the mainland. One wrinkle in the plan may be that there is unexploded ordnance buried on Nomans Land (get it?), since it was once used for military training. Biologist Eileen McGourty, who helped with the release, said the bombs should not be a danger to the rabbits, who are much too light to set them off. A full-grown biologist, on the other hand, may be another matter. "We follow safety guidelines when on the island," McGourty says, adding that the explosives will always be a danger to humans.

In Japan, meanwhile, the two islands the Amami rabbit calls home, Amami-Oshima and Tokuno-Shima, are seeing a promising return of the lagomorphs. This comes four decades after officials introduced mongooses onto the islands, hoping they would control the venomous snakes who were biting their way across the landscape. But the mongoose population expanded rapidly and seemed to avoid the snakes altogether, showing instead a preference for the rabbits, whose numbers quickly declined. To save the Amami and some other native species, the country's Ministry of the Environment began targeting the mongooses in 2005, which is sad in its own right. The situation has greatly improved for the Amami rabbits, however, as in the near absence of predators their population grew from a few thousand in 2003 to perhaps as many as 40,000 by 2019. In addition to being named national treasures in Japan, the Amami are rare among rabbits for their vocalization, a loud call that can now be heard more frequently in the forests of Amami-Oshima and Tokuno-Shima.

World's Largest Known Bunny

In 1989, paleontologist Josep Quintana of the Institut Català de Paleontologia in Barcelona was digging on the small island of Minorca, which was at one time connected to Spain, when he thought he'd found the remains of a giant turtle. After years of careful work, he announced in 2011 that what he'd found was actually the fossilized skeleton of a prehistoric rabbit. This lagomorph, which Dr. Quintana named *Nuralagus rex*—"King of the Minorcan Rabbits"—was about 26 pounds (12 kg) when they roamed the island three to five million years ago. That's around six times bigger than the average bunny we see today. What is remarkable about this rabbit isn't just their size (though a bunny with the approximate dimensions of a full-grown Irish Setter is indeed impressive) but how different their anatomy was. In an example of what paleontologists refer to as "insular gigantism" and evolutionary biologists call "island rule," *N. rex* had no predators, leading them to grow large bodies with small ears and small eyes, thus losing the acute senses of hearing and sight mainland rabbits possess. They also lost their fleet-footed mobility, since there was no need for them to run from anyone. Alas, they still became extinct.

Also uncommon is the legal protection granted to the Amami rabbit, banning the trapping and hunting of these animals, which are just two of the ways rabbits are exploited around the world. The use of rabbits in general as a source of food, however, is closely linked with how we ultimately sought them out as friends and family members. It was the farmers' children and wives, after all, who were most likely the first to view rabbits as more than an economic resource and at least grant them some affection, if not bond with them outright. It is certainly not difficult to imagine how easily a child surrounded by farmed animals would grow especially fond of a particular rabbit and wish to keep them as a playmate. This is where the rabbit–human relationship probably began in earnest.

We've come a long way since then. Today, many rabbit advocacy groups tout them as the third most popular companion animal in the United States, and that may very well be. But the truth is the statistics we have on rabbits are not as reliable as those for dogs and cats (which are really just best guesses, anyway) because breeders, animal shelters, and veterinarians are not necessarily required to keep track. I suspect this is a holdover from the less-enlightened days when the intrinsic value of rabbits was measured on a weight scale, not by their incalculable worth as individuals with needs and wants of their own.

One thing is certain, however, which is that more and more people are embracing rabbits as companion animals who are not relegated to an outdoor hutch but live inside the home. This is especially the case in urban areas, where flora and fauna are vanishing and living with a house rabbit is often seen (or subconsciously felt) as a connection with the last vestiges of what is untamed as our dwindling natural landscape is bulldozed to make way for shopping malls and parking garages. The domesticated rabbit may be vastly different from their rustic cousins—much more likely to run to humans for a treat than to retreat out of fear—but compared to canines and felines, that domestication is relatively recent, giving the rabbit an additional aura of "wild" mystique.

Chapter Two

Leporine Lore

The rabbit would not give up. The fire would be his.
"For am I not the biggest, finest, and handsomest rabbit that people have ever seen?" the rabbit said.
The next year, the rabbit went to the Green Corn Dance. It was not easy for the rabbit to get the people to trust him, but they did.
—Seminole legend

Long before scientific pursuits such as astronomy or biology or mathematics attempted to make sense of the universe, before philosophy or theology tried to answer crucial questions about existence, humans were seeking to understand the natural world through the animals with whom they lived in close contact. Among some Native American cultures, for instance, the bison was associated with fertility and controlled how many children a woman would have. According to the creation myth of Finland, the land, sun, moon, and stars were formed from eggs laid by a beautiful seabird. The Kuba peoples of Central Africa tell of a deity called Mbombo who vomited nine animals, and they in turn created all the world's creatures.

Virtually every animal has found a place within folklore and mythology, with each culture emphasizing the qualities of the animal they admired or feared. And when an animal is as geographically widespread as the rabbit or the hare—who are often treated as interchangeable by societies that only have one or the other—it is no surprise to find them featured in so many legends. It is not only the rabbit's ubiquity that makes them the focus of myths; they also possess characteristics that lend themselves to fabled interpretation. Take the rabbit's admittedly eerie habit of sleeping with their eyes open from time to time. While there is a perfectly reasonable explanation for this evolutionary feat (self-defense), ancient Britons, Egyptians, and Romans inferred that rabbits had the ability to observe everything, such as the outcome of future battles. Fortifying their supernatural reputation is the rabbit's practice of digging and living in burrows, which was perceived by some as giving rabbits the power to communicate with spirits of the underworld.

With their fleeting moments aboveground, relying on their wits as they do, rabbits embody much of what humans have come to appreciate in other animals. Rabbits and hares are associated with spring, the moon, rejuvenation, and fertility, and so they are often thought to bring good luck. It was once believed that glimpsing a rabbit or hare in your field, for example, meant that you were going to have an especially abundant harvest or that it was an auspicious time to have a child. For the Romans, rabbits were a traditional gift intended to help a woman conceive. Ancient Egyptians revered the protective goddess Wenet (sometimes spelled Unut), who was depicted as having the head of a rabbit. In ancient Greece, the hare was sacred to Aphrodite, the goddess of love, beauty, and sexuality. Hermes, the messenger of the Olympian gods, so respected the swiftness of hares that he created the constellation Lepus in their honor. (Here are some fun facts for your next trivia night: The brightest star in Lepus is 14 times the mass of the sun and goes by various names, including Arneb, derived from the Arabic word for "hare," while in Chinese astronomy, the stars of Lepus comprise a surprisingly different constellation: Cè, meaning "toilet.")

Bad Omens

Superstition can be a tricky business, and not everyone believed rabbits and hares were good luck. One tradition, for instance, held that seeing a hare or rabbit could portend a major fire in your village, while another example of misfortune maintained that if a hare crossed the path of a fisherman on his way to the water, he would catch nothing that day. Indeed, hares seemed to have a particularly sinister reputation among fishermen in many cultures, and they wouldn't even board a boat if they saw a hare — bad for them but good for the fishes, so maybe this wasn't such bad luck after all.

Because of their cunning and need to keep one step ahead of everyone for their survival, rabbits are also frequently represented as tricksters in ancient stories.

Within a 2500-year-old collection of Hindu fables called *The Panchatantra* is a tale that illustrates this beautifully. It seems a certain lion was terrorizing the jungle, indiscriminately eating animals left and right. Not surprisingly, the critters thought this situation was intolerable. They decided to appease the lion and promised to bring him an animal each day, but in return, the lion was to stay at home. The lion wouldn't have to labor for his food, so he agreed. This arrangement worked fine until it was the rabbit's turn to become lunch. The rabbit took his time reaching the lion's den, which angered the lion, who did not like to be kept waiting for his daily meal. When the rabbit finally arrived, the lion was really worked up. Not only was his meal overdue, he thought, but it's so small! "How dare you arrive so late!" he growled. The clever rabbit was apologetic and explained that a new lion claiming to be the *real* king of the jungle had delayed him and caused his tardiness. Enraged, the lion demanded that the rabbit take him to see this lion who dared challenge his reign. "He is strong and lives in a fortress," warned the rabbit, who agreed to lead the lion to his rival's home. They walked together to the other side of the jungle, where the rabbit pointed to a circular stone wall. "He resides inside that citadel," he said. The lion climbed the wall, peered over the top, and saw another lion looking back at him. The lion did not realize he was seeing his own image reflected in the water of a deep well. He roared at the usurper, and his roar echoed in response. "Wow, you weren't kidding," said the lion to the rabbit. "This fellow looks strong, and his roar is mighty. But I will make short work of him." At that the lion jumped into the well, never to return. The other animals were understandably quite pleased by this turn of events and, it must be imagined, there was much rejoicing in the jungle.

This mythic story is one of many found worldwide depicting smaller animals outsmarting larger, more physically imposing ones. (They don't call it "outfoxing" for nothing.) In a Tibetan version of this tale, the lion is looking for a daily show of respect from the other animals, not a meal. But a certain rabbit is quite relaxed on a bed of soft grass one morning, feeling far too comfortable to be bothered with visiting the lion. When the angry lion spots him, the rabbit is sure he's about to be killed, so he thinks fast, telling the lion that he was on his way to make his obeisance to him when he came to a stream and in it was an imposing demon. "I was afraid," the rabbit says, "and ran up here a few minutes ago to hide in this grass." The lion wants to know more about this demon. According to the rabbit, the demon is eager to challenge the lion's reign as king and is ready to do battle with him. Angrier than ever, the ferocious feline follows the rabbit to the stream, where he mistakes his reflection for the face of the "demon" and jumps into the water, drowning.

Many of these fables may not exactly make for the most peaceful bedtime reading today, but they were originally passed down from one generation to the next through the spoken word, and the lessons were powerful.

Rabbits also figure prominently in many Native American traditions. One of my favorite stories is the Menominee myth of the rabbit who created day and night. As the narrative unfolds, a rabbit hero named Manabush (literally "Great Rabbit") is traveling through the forest under a dark sky. He calls up to an owl perched in a tree, telling him he doesn't like the dark and is going to make it light. The owl, thinking the rabbit is a fool, tells him to go ahead and try, then suggests instead that they have a contest to see who is stronger; the winner can have the world either in darkness or light, as it suits him. All the animals of the forest—some preferring light and others preferring dark—come to witness the contest as the rabbit begins chanting, "Light, light, light," and the owl recites, "Night, night, night." If one makes a mistake and repeats the other's word, he loses. Eventually the owl slips up and says "Light." Oops. The rabbit wins the privilege of choosing perpetual daylight. But he decides to have both darkness and light, for the benefit of all. Everyone in the forest is happy, and no one gets hurt.

I admire this story for its central theme of compromise. Manabush could have chosen to have things his way, but instead he considered the needs and wishes of all the animals. We can also read deeper meaning in this legend when we know that rabbits are crepuscular—that is, they are most active in those moments when day transitions to night (dusk) and night to day (dawn). Light therefore plays an important role in the life of these animals, as the Menominee surely recognized and respected.

Another Native American legend, this one from the Seminole peoples of present-day Florida, explains how a rabbit helped humans obtain the secret of fire. As the tale is told, only one tribe had the power of fire, and they would not share it. Every year during the Green Corn Ceremony—an annual festival celebrating the corn harvest—the Indians danced around a large fire lit by the holders of the secret. Members of other tribes tried to learn the secret but could never get close enough to the fire. At one ceremony, the finest and handsomest rabbit the Indians had ever seen begged to be allowed to dance with them around the fire. He was permitted to dance and got close enough to grab a burning stick from the fire and ran off with it. But the tribe called forth rain and extinguished the fire-stick. Undeterred, the rabbit returned the following year, again charmed his way into being allowed to dance, and again he escaped with a burning stick. Medicine men from the tribe created a rainstorm to put out the fire-stick. The same events unfold the following year. But in his fourth attempt, the rabbit hides the burning stick beneath a rocky ledge, thus keeping the flame lit when the rain comes. He then shares the secret of fire with the other tribes.

The Iroquois, meanwhile, tell of two hunters who went into the forest and heard a loud thump. Looking into a clearing, they saw that the source of the sound was a large rabbit, who continued to thump the ground with his back foot. Then, from all directions, smaller rabbits hopped into the clearing. As the hunters watched transfixed, the large rabbit rhythmically thumped while the little rabbits danced to the beat. The two men ran back to the village and told the elders what they had seen. One elder asks the hunters to demonstrate the dance, and so they show them. Another elder says the rabbits have given the villagers this dance so the tribe could show appreciation to the rabbit people for all they give them. And so the Iroquois honor rabbits with the Rabbit Dance at social gatherings.

The Mysterious Horned Hare

A uniquely North American bit of lagomorph lore centers on the jackalope, a mythical hare or sometimes a rabbit topped with antlers. Unlike most lagomorphs, however, the rarely seen jackalope is said to aggressively attack people, giving the creature the nickname "warrior rabbit." Stories about the jackalope have been around for centuries, perhaps most famously linked to the explorer John Colter, who supposedly encountered one during the Lewis and Clark Expedition in 1807 or 1808. The legend took on new life in the 1930s, when a couple of Wyoming taxidermists created a jackalope as a hoax and then made them for sale. The jackalope image soon became a regular fixture on postcards, bumper stickers, T-shirts, and other memorabilia. As is common with myths, the jackalope has some basis in reality: many wild rabbits have a viral infection called Shope's papilloma that results in growths that look like horns or antlers; it's not difficult to imagine someone observing a cottontail with horn-like tumors and concluding they had spotted a legendary jackalope.

Rabbits take on a distinctly different role in the Aztec myth of the Centzon Totochtin, in which they are celebrated as gods of inebriation. Meaning "four hundred rabbits," though really understood as "infinite rabbits," the Centzon Totochtin get drunk on a viscous, fermented agave beverage called pulque, which has been imbibed in Mesoamerica for at least a thousand years. The rabbits represent the various effects of drinking pulque in excess—angry, sad, chatty, pushy, beer-goggled, and so on—and they are all said to be the offspring of Mayahuel, the goddess of alcohol. Although not every one of the rabbit deities has a name, their leader is Ome Tochtli, or "Two Rabbit," who is associated with both drunkenness and fertility, which have had an indisputable relationship throughout history. Papaztac ("The Enervated") is the god of foam. Macuil Tochtli ("Five Rabbit") is the god of hangovers and seems directly linked with Quatlapanqui ("Head Splitter").

In other mythic traditions, the rabbit (or hare) is closely associated with feminine principles and the moon—which, like the sun, is also a marker of time but intimately connected with women. There is arguably no better example of this symbiosis than the Chinese goddess Chang'e, who floated up to the moon after drinking an immortality elixir and enjoyed a lunar life (a very long one, it must be said) with her friend, Jade Rabbit. A harvest deity who oversees not only the fruitfulness of the land but also the lives and loves of women, Chang'e is said to endow her worshippers with beauty.

Jade Rabbit has an interesting backstory. Evidently, one day a figure known as the Jade Emperor, the highest ruler of heaven and the gods, disguised himself as a poor, elderly man and set out to beg for food from the animals of Earth. A monkey, an otter, and a jackal all collected suitable food for him. But the rabbit was only experienced in gathering grass, which he knew humans do not eat, so with a boldness that goes well beyond any etiquette for being a good host, he threw himself onto a fire so that he could offer his own body as nourishment. Fear not, though, because the rabbit was not harmed, and suddenly—like a magician pulling a you-know-who from his hat—the man revealed himself to be the all-powerful Jade Emperor. Deeply moved by the rabbit's virtue and self-sacrifice, he sent him to the moon to dwell forever as the Jade Rabbit.

Nearly identical to this fable is one from the Buddhist tradition, except in this version, the rabbit tells his friends—the monkey, the otter, and the jackal—that the next full moon will herald a holy day, and any beggars should be given food. It is the Buddha in the guise of a wandering mendicant who pulls him from the fire before he comes to any harm and, depending on the variation told, either sends him to the moon or simply carves the virtuous rabbit's image onto the lunar surface to remind the world of his act of compassion. (In some accounts the rabbit even shakes free the insects in his fur, to spare them from the flames.) The Buddhist myth was almost certainly adapted into the Jade Rabbit story, as well as one told in Japan in which the Old Man of the Moon appears on Earth disguised as a pauper and asks a fox, a monkey, and a rabbit for a hot meal, with the now-familiar outcome.

These narratives are also strikingly similar to one told centuries ago in Mesoamerica, in which the god Quetzalcoatl is living on Earth as a man. As he walks across a desert, the sky becomes dark and Quetzalcoatl grows so hungry that he sits down, finally noticing a rabbit munching on his dinner nearby. "What are you eating?" he asks the rabbit. "Grass," comes the reply. "Would you like some?" "No, not really," says Quetzalcoatl, who adds that he will probably die of starvation. The rabbit then offers his own body as food, acknowledging that he is very small, but at least the meager repast will help satisfy the man's hunger. Quetzalcoatl is so heartened by the rabbit's compassion that he reveals himself to be a god, lifts him up, imprints the rabbit's image onto the moon, and brings him down again. "You may be small," he says, "but your portrait on the moon will forever tell the story of your kindness." (Oh, here's another fun fact: Many mythologists believe that the rabbit is associated with the moon because the animal's gestation period is about 30 days—the same length as a lunar cycle.)

After reading about these myths from China, Tibet, Japan, and Mesoamerica, you may be wondering, as I was, how they could share so many archetypes. I mean, how does a story in which a rabbit, the moon, and a supernatural being interact to achieve the same result spring from such far-flung corners of the globe? Well, it turns out this kind of mythological consistency happens a lot; in fact, it is so widespread that folklorists have a name for it—two names, actually. The first, *polygenesis*, is a fancy way of saying that congruent storylines were created independently, since mythic storytelling comes from beliefs and customs that are common to peoples of the same stages of culture. But wait, not so fast, say other scholars, who endorse the philosophy of *diffusionism*, which holds that a story was created in one location and then spread geographically over time through migration. Proponents of this viewpoint contend that the polygenesis theory has to be wrong because humans are simply not that smart, and when you remember that we are the species responsible for such ideas as trophy hunting, clamato juice, and the selfie stick, you must admit they have a point.

Forgive my tangent on where these myths came from, but I believe they say something important about how humans have felt toward and interacted with rabbits. Consider another mythic image from Mesoamerica in which Ixchel, the Mayan moon goddess, is depicted sitting on a crescent moon with a rabbit in her arms. She is venerated as the goddess of marriage, procreation, and childbirth. Like the Chinese moon goddess Chang'e, she is also a harvest deity who is associated with the fertility of crops and vegetation. It is easy to see how a culture would notice the rabbit's (or hare's) intimate connection to the land and their monthly cycle of rebirth and create fundamental traditions around them to help shape the people's worldview. Moreover, because these animals are geographically diverse, it makes sense that so many different cultures would adopt (and adapt) the rabbit into their mythic storytelling. And it's no stretch to suppose that more people today look up at the nighttime orb and interpret its dark shapes and craters as, not a man in the moon, but the silhouette of a rabbit.

Lagomorphs are deeply connected to the moon in other cultures as well. The Norse fertility and lunar goddess Freyja has an entourage of hares. In Siberia, the shapeshifting moon goddess Kaltes appears as a hare and is closely associated with childbirth and rejuvenation. Among the rare examples of a male lunar deity is the Egyptian god Osiris, who sometimes goes about his divine business disguised as a hare.

St. Melangell and the Hare
Nestled near the head of a deep glacial valley in the picturesque Welsh village of Llangynog, just off an

impossibly narrow road, is a small church containing the oldest Romanesque shrine in northern Europe. The church and shrine honor St. Melangell (she died about 590), who fled Ireland in the sixth century to escape a forced marriage, took a vow of celibacy, and settled into a quiet, solitary life in Wales, where she remained in divine seclusion for 15 years, evidently sleeping on a bare rock. It is said that fate intervened in the form of a hare being pursued by a local prince and his hunting dogs. The hare sought asylum beneath Melangell's cloak, and when his royal highness demanded to have the hare, she refused. Duly impressed with her compassion and piety, the prince gave Melangell the valley as a sanctuary for animals, and she became the abbess of a small religious community there. Pennant Melangell Church is filled with many depictions of hares—even on her grave marker in the churchyard— and is a pilgrimage site for Christians and lagomorph lovers alike. It will come as no surprise that Melangell is the patron saint of hares and rabbits.

Even as we examine narratives that might blur the line between tale and truth, we get a glimpse of the reverence people have for lagomorphs. When the Roman dictator Julius Caesar invaded the British Isles in 54 BCE, he reported that the Celtic peoples considered it taboo to eat hares (mountain hares, to be specific; the Romans would later introduce rabbits and brown hares to Britain). This could have been due to a local Druid belief that female seers could shapeshift into hares under the moonlight or because hares were closely associated with goddesses and were believed to have supernatural powers. Historians now disagree about whether Caesar's observation was an accurate portrayal of the dining preferences of the early Britons, but two things are indisputably true: many Celts considered the hare to be magical or even sacred, and some people do eat hares and rabbits.

What is important here is not so much the specific names or even the dates, but that as a consequence of being raised for food, rabbits were in close proximity with humans, and we began to regard them as more than a meal—and, indeed, more than a myth.

Chapter Three

The Legacy of Eostre

Easter Bunny, Easter Bunny,
When oh when are you coming?
Hop around and let me see
All the treats you have for me.
Chocolate eggs are best of all,
Even if they're very small.
—*Lieber, Lieber Osterhase* (A German Easter song)

If there were a Venn diagram illustrating the relationship among rabbits, folklore, and the festival known by many people as Easter, its central overlapping intersection would be labeled "Easter Bunny," and that section would most likely be highlighted in pastel yellow. It would seem that not only do rabbits and Easter go together like peanut butter and jam but that it's been so for centuries. Well, not quite.

In a world where religious customs have become increasingly mainstream, Easter has resisted the kind of secularization that has conquered Christmas and Halloween—we don't ordinarily attend office Easter parties, for instance, nor has the Easter rom-com become a popular film genre. As a secular symbol, however, the Easter Bunny is arguably more associated with the holiday than any religious image. The Bunny has even become something akin to Santa Claus: a tool for parents to coax pleasant behavior from children who hope to be treated to sweets and presents bestowed by an otherworldly emissary of goodwill.

Theories abound about how and when a gift-giving rabbit came to be associated with this Christian holiday. One hypothesis that is frequently cited concerns a definitely-non-Christian goddess of spring named Eostre, who may or may not have had a cult following in ancient Britain and whose sacred animal is said to be a rabbit or hare. Some authors have claimed that Eostre didn't just socialize with lagomorphs but was actually part leporine herself—specifically, that her head was that of a hare—but others argue such suggestions are revivalist neopaganism firmly rooted in the twentieth century. Modern books on paganism associate Eostre with Druids and Wiccans and declare without hesitation that "Eostre's totem animal was the rabbit."

An intriguing point about the link between Eostre and hares springs from Germany's Rhineland, said to be home to a cult that worshipped the goddess and the place from which brown hares were exported to Britain. In other words, the same location is regarded as being responsible for introducing both Eostre and the animal associated with her, which seems like an extraordinary coincidence. The most reliable historical evidence we have for the existence of Eostre worship, at least for the moment, is from the Venerable Bede, a Benedictine monk who wrote briefly about her in the eighth century. He makes no reference linking her to any animals, however, let alone lagomorphs.

Many historians contend that Bede simply fabricated her from whole cloth and even argue that Eostre's Germanic parallel, the goddess Ostara, is a name that folklorist Jacob Grimm created in 1835. I'm sorry if this news spoils any fond childhood memories (assuming you were raised in a pagan household), but I find it's best to be honest, especially as it pertains to rabbits. That isn't to say we can't enjoy Easter bunnies with gusto, or Anglo-Saxon goddesses, for that matter; they just don't seem to be related.

Not that popular culture hasn't tried to connect them.

Every spring there are stories in the mainstream media and open-minded church newsletters claiming that today's Easter Bunny is a leftover from the vernal equinox festival of Eostre, whose symbol was the hare or rabbit, and that she oversaw such important matters in the ancient world as fertility, the rising sun, and the ripening of fruit—though, again, there's no historical record anywhere to account for this. "All the stuff about dawn and hares and everything else is entirely speculation," says Martha Bayless, director of folklore and public culture at the University of Oregon. She estimates that only about 15 percent of what's written about Eostre might be true. "But which 15 percent? Nobody knows. That's the trouble with academics—saying what's actually known, as opposed to what is speculation, is much less interesting."

Ronald Hutton, professor of history at the University of Bristol and an expert on paganism and British folklore, is equally skeptical, contending that Eostre didn't become associated with rabbits or hares until the twentieth century. "First the great nineteenth-century German scholar Jacob Grimm suggested that if the English word 'Easter' derived from 'Eostre,' then the medieval German equivalent for the festival, 'Ostara,' must have derived from a German spring goddess with that name," he says. "Linguists now think that Ostara derives instead from the Anglo-Saxon 'Easter,' and there is no evidence for a goddess called Ostara." Regardless, says Dr. Hutton, non-academic readers of Grimm accepted her completely and linked her to hares. "That association then got transferred to Eostre at some point in the mid to late twentieth century."

The theory of Eostre being linked to lagomorphs only in the twentieth century is a common one, but Stephen Winick, a writer and editor at the Library of Congress's American Folklife Center, disagrees with this suggestion. Writing on the Library's website in 2016, Winick traces the Eostre–hare connection to at least as far back as 1883, when the English journal *Folk-Lore* published a commentary by one H. Krebs who in turn cited a German book by K. A. Oberle from that same year that mentions Eostre changing a bird into a hare. The mammal is then able to thank her for what must certainly have been a monumental inconvenience by laying a clutch of colorful eggs on her festival at Eastertime. (Eggs are a widespread symbol of rebirth and resurrection and given as gifts in many cultures.)

Winick believes that Oberle got the idea of Eostre turning a bird into a hare from Adolf Holtzmann, who wrote about the Easter Hare in 1874. But Holtzmann never said that Eostre had magically turned a bird into a hare, only that the hare must have once been a bird; in other words, he may have simply meant that Eostre had an avian companion before having a leporine companion. But Oberle took the story a leap beyond, stating that Eostre unequivocally used her divine powers to *transform* a bird into a hare. So why, wondered Winick, did Oberle take such editorial license with Holzmann's story? "He likely did this because his book was specifically intended to argue for survivals of paganism in Christian Germany, and giving the Easter Hare a definitively pagan origin served this scholarly agenda," Winick writes. "In adding this element, Oberle provided the essence of the current popular stories."

Regardless of her origins, the goddess has become a veritable cash machine for the Earth religions market.

None of this is to suggest that rabbits and hares have not been connected to springtime for thousands of years. Nor do I mean to malign paganism, which, truth be told, I find much more sensible and appealing than many other belief systems. Any religion that centers nature in its tradition, for example, is all right by me. But if we're going to pin this tale onto one figure from antiquity, there should at least be some historical basis for the connection beyond the word of Bede, whose task it was to suppress polytheism.

Whatever Eostre's place in history, it seems probable that

Easter was named after her—Bede stated that the Anglo-Saxons called April *Eosturmonath*, or "Easter month," and celebrated with feasts in her honor. We must also acknowledge the important role rabbits and hares have played in ancient religious ceremonies. Writing in the journal *Folk-Lore* in 1892, translator Charles Billson observed that "whether there ever was a goddess named Eostre, or not, and whatever connection the hare may have had with the ritual of Saxon or British worship, there are good grounds for believing that the sacredness of this animal reaches back into an age still more remote, when it probably played a very important part at the great Spring Festival of the prehistoric inhabitants of this island."

So where does the Easter Bunny tradition come from, if not Eostre? In a project aptly named Easter E.g. (e.g. as in "example"), researchers from England's Oxford University, the University of Exeter, the University of Leicester, and the University of Nottingham traced the history of the Easter Bunny to its roots as a kind of test case to better understand how ideas become accepted by the mainstream—especially ideas that are not native to a given country. Why is it, they wondered, that old ideas from other cultures—such as Christianity, introduced by the Romans—are accepted and even nostalgic, while recently imported ideas are considered "alien" and "invasive"? The answers could help us understand shifting attitudes on religion, conservation, and even nationalism.

The Easter Bunny makes a good case study since the animals associated with the Christian celebration of Easter—namely, rabbits, brown hares, and chicks—are not native to England, but because they migrated to Britain sometime in the long-forgotten past, they are fondly embraced as part of the British identity. (In contrast to the Easter Bunny, newer arrivals onto the British Isles—such as the "Americanized" version of Halloween, with costumed children going door to door in search of candy—are frowned upon.) Ancient communities often believed animals from remote realms possessed powerful, even supernatural, qualities. It's easy to see how the introduction of Christianity could have resulted in the "exotic" rabbit becoming a symbol of early religious festivals.

"What we're trying to show with our Easter project is these kinds of introduced ideas have been happening for millennia," says Naomi Sykes, professor of archeology at the University of Exeter and principal investigator in the study. "We just accept other ones because they happened a long, long time ago, like Christianity. The same is true with a lot of the animals we see. So long as the animals were introduced a long time ago, we accept them as morally part of our wildlife. But anything that's come in recent years, such as grey squirrels [brought to Britain in the 1870s], are disliked and people want to see them eradicated. It's a way of thinking about ideas through animals."

Researchers with the Easter E.g. project have determined that the Easter Bunny as a symbol is not that old, at least in the context of human history. Luke John Murphy, an historical linguist at the University of Leicester, says the Easter Bunny originated in northern Germany, probably sometime in the sixteenth or seventeenth century. "He didn't start out as a bunny; he started out as a hare," he says. "And it was as a hare, which he still is in Germany, that he gets imported to Great Britain." Dr. Murphy adds that the Easter Hare had displaced an earlier symbol, the Easter Fox (*Osterfuchs*), a character possibly inspired by the fox's habit of stealing and burying eggs.

What animal may have preceded the fox as an Easter figure is anyone's guess, says Philip A. Shaw, senior lecturer in English language at the University of Leicester. "We don't really know what the original Easter animal was—or even if there was just one, original Easter animal—but it's true that there are traditions involving other animals besides the hare." Yet he agrees it was the hare who appears to have hopped from the European continent to the British Isles. "References to the Easter Hare in Britain seem to begin appearing in the nineteenth century and are usually mentioned as German traditions at the time, which tempts me to suppose that this may have been another German tradition, like the Christmas tree, introduced by the Victorians," he says.

One possible explanation for the Easter Bunny supplanting the Easter Hare as a symbol in Great Britain is linked to hares being widely hunted in the country. The decline of hare numbers in the nineteenth century coincided with an increase in the rabbit population, which occurred as Easter was becoming a common Victorian tradition.

Complicating the challenge of tracing the Easter Bunny's history in England is that it's very difficult to differentiate ancient symbols of the mountain hare, which is native to the Scottish Highlands; the brown hare, which probably arrived in Britain during the Early/Middle Iron Age (800–100 BCE), possibly from Germany; and the rabbit. Rabbits were first introduced into Britain by the Romans in the first century, but that initial population didn't become established, leading to another introduction sometime in the late twelfth or early thirteenth century—though from where has yet to be confirmed. Figuring out these lagomorph timelines can be tricky, as well. Because rabbits burrow deep underground, archeologists find their bones resting amid layers of soil that date to periods earlier than the skeletons are actually from. "It's a nightmare," says Dr. Sykes, "and I think it's one reason there has been so little research done on rabbits—in Britain, at least."

Despite being non-natives, rabbits and brown hares are well loved in the British Isles. "In Britain, you have this incredible cultural connection to the brown hare, especially, and then to the rabbit on top of that," says the University of Exeter's Carly Ameen, an archeological scientist specializing in zooarcheology. "People like Beatrix Potter have made it an icon—Peter Rabbit, and all these things. At the same time, there is this underlying symbol of rabbits and hares that represent something bigger about the way that we identify culturally what is native to us and what is alien."

The Easter Bilby

Because rabbits are frowned upon by many in Australia, they have the Easter Bilby, a desert-dwelling marsupial who happens to be endangered. Money raised from sales of certain bilby-shaped chocolates supports conservation efforts.

While our knowledge of how rabbits and the Easter Bunny migrated to Great Britain is currently limited, exploring these chronologies through the lens of archeology promises some exciting insights. "The history of Easter has never really been studied using archeology before, which is why we don't yet understand the connections between the natural and cultural history of the real-life animals and that of the Easter Bunny," explains Thomas Fowler, professor of archeology at the University of Nottingham. "Examining ancient hare and rabbit bones and the cultural setting we find them in allows us to learn more about when these animals arrived, and how humans have interacted with them through time," such as our early perceptions of them and how—or if—we managed their populations. "If we can bring all this together with evidence from artifacts, genetics, history, et cetera, we'll arrive at a completely new understanding of how and why the Easter Bunny became part of our culture."

The Easter E.g. project did not examine how the Easter Bunny reached the United States, but some historians speculate that the tradition made its way across the Atlantic on eighteenth-century voyages with German immigrants, who settled in Pennsylvania. They brought with them tales and customs of the *Osterhase* or

Oschter Haws ("Easter Hare"), who distributed eggs to well-behaved children. Hare-shaped cakes were baked to add some sweetness to the festivities. Easter Bunny rituals eventually spread across the country, augmented by candy-filled baskets, Easter Bunny songs, and fires. Yes, fires. The Texas town of Fredericksburg has a tradition that supposedly dates back to an evening in 1847, when German immigrants were said to be negotiating a treaty with Comanche Indians, who signaled one another in the hills with fire. Some of the immigrants then told their children that the flames were lit by the Easter Hare, and he was using them to boil eggs. But the Germans actually have a much older custom of using Eastertime fires to celebrate the end of winter—a practice Jacob Grimm wrote about in the same 1835 book in which he mentions the goddess Ostara—so it did not begin in Fredericksburg.

Names for the long-eared patron of Easter transformed during the nineteenth century, with the "Easter Hare" giving way to the "Easter Rabbit" in the USA, where one of the earliest print references can be found. An 1877 article in Ohio's *Belmont Chronicle* describes the connection between Easter eggs and rabbits, explaining that "on Easter morning it is the duty and pleasure of all to hunt for the Easter nests to see what the Easter rabbit has laid for them, he surely having visited the house that night, laying them some lovely Easter presents for all good little children." By the early 1890s, newspapers were using "Easter-bunny" to signify the furry purveyor of colored eggs, and plushy rabbit toys were being marketed as "Easter Bunnies," and all of these signaled a gradual shift from "Easter Rabbit" to "Easter Bunny" in advertisements and popular culture over the next several decades.

As with most legends, the folklore surrounding Easter and rabbits owes much to how people interpret nature. One theory about the role of eggs during this holiday is traced to the

English countryside, the grassy fields of which are home to both hares and birds called lapwings (or sometimes plovers), whose call and tumbling aerial courtship displays herald the arrival of spring. Because lapwings make their nests in a shallow indentation in the soil, their eggs are easy pickings for predators, among the most voracious of whom are humans. Reputedly rich and delicious, the eggs were collected by adults and children for hundreds of years and were said to be a favorite of Queen Victoria. (The Protection of Lapwings Act, passed in 1926, has since halted killing the birds for food or taking their eggs.)

Hares also nest on the ground, in depressions called forms, and it's not uncommon for them to borrow an unsupervised lapwing nest or take cover there should the need arise. In turn, a mama lapwing will quite happily use a hare's nest to lay her eggs. (Likewise, puffins and shearwaters have been known to evict rabbits from their burrows, using their powerful beaks, if necessary.) With all this interspecies nest-swapping, it's not difficult to imagine that England's country folk might disturb a hare in a nest, find a clutch of eggs, and conclude that hares lay eggs. And it's easy to see how the collection of these eggs in the tall grass could lead to the popular tradition of the Easter egg hunt. Indeed, an 1890 article in *The Scots Observer* explicitly describes the custom of collecting lapwing's eggs on Easter as a "hunt." It seems that by this time, at least, readers understood hares didn't lay eggs.

Since there is apparently no such thing as an original idea—or perhaps as another example of either polygenesis or diffusionism—let us turn back for a moment to Germany's *Osterhase*, who was not only a purveyor of eggs but was also considered their biological source. The tale was first recorded in 1682 by a young physician named Johannes Richier, but he was warning against eating the eggs, which he believed would make children sick. Of the tradition, he writes: "In Alsace and neighboring regions, these eggs are called hare's eggs because of the myth told to fool simple people and children that the Easter Hare laid the eggs to hatch hidden in the garden's grass, bushes, etc., where they are eagerly sought out by the children to the delight of the smiling adults."

The German custom undoubtedly predates the seventeenth century and is often linked to stories about a poor woman who decorated eggs and hid them in a garden for kids to find. Upon seeing a hare or two nearby (certainly not an exceptional sight in a garden), children assumed that they had laid the eggs, and the mythological mammal known as the *Osterhase* was born, gradually replacing the Easter Fox (*Osterfuchs*).

Yet another natural observation relevant to the lagomorph–Easter connection is that hares, who lead generally solitary lives throughout most of the year, become more social in early spring. This is when they can be seen engaging in a mating ritual that finds males chasing females, the two of them leaping into the air and "boxing" each other. The apparently erratic behavior inspired the expression "mad as a March hare," and this memorable display by hares in the fields, like the courtship of lapwings in the sky, would have told Europeans that the seasons were changing and Easter was close at hand.

Even in the twenty-first century, it seems the public still hasn't quite figured out lagomorph reproduction. According to Google, each year around Easter the search engine sees a huge spike in the query "Do rabbits lay eggs?" Perhaps that's not terribly surprising, considering 7 percent of adults in the United States—about 18 million people—believe that chocolate milk comes from brown cows. Seriously. Eostre's mythical rabbit laid eggs, as we have seen, but at least that rabbit was a bird to begin with.

Chapter Four

Lagomorph Lexicon and Literature

Once upon a time there were four little Rabbits.
—Beatrix Potter, *The Tale of Peter Rabbit*

Deep within the historic market town of Beverley in northern England is a lovely Anglican church called St. Mary's. Founded in 1120, St. Mary's is the oldest building in the city and is known for its beautiful Norman architecture and ornate ceilings. But this church's real claim to fame may be the stone sculpture of a rabbit (or hare) on one side of a chapel archway. The 18-inch (45-cm) rabbit, looking rather pleased with himself, carries a staff and a satchel and dates to about 1330. Although some online sources link the sculpture with a fable by Odo of Cheriton, the church has christened the figure "the pilgrim rabbit" and believes it represents the many religious travelers whose offerings helped make Beverley one of the wealthiest medieval towns in the country. The especially long ears of the sculpture are one reason scholars believe it was more likely a hare that the artist had in mind, although the church itself seems divided on the subject. St. Mary's newsletter is called *The Pilgrim Rabbit*, but an article within a 2019 issue takes a theological approach in arguing the lagomorph depicted must be a hare: "For a hare was believed to modestly back up to its mate and put its trust in God rather than in lust in order to reproduce. A rabbit was considered to be far more promiscuous with less holy habits than the hare."

What makes the sculpture famous is not any discussion of

rabbit or hare piety but the local legend that it served as a model for the White Rabbit character in Lewis Carroll's 1865 book *Alice's Adventures in Wonderland*. It is possible that Carroll saw the sculpture as a youth when his family visited the area, and its similarity to John Tenniel's drawings of the White Rabbit for the novel is indeed remarkable. The city even promotes the notion that the author sent Tenniel to St. Mary's specifically to study the sculpture for inspiration.

While we can't be sure if Lewis Carroll ever saw the pilgrim rabbit, without a doubt he created one of the most enduring rabbits (and hares) in literary history. The White Rabbit signifies not just someone perpetually in a hurry but also Alice's quest for knowledge; he is the very catalyst that sparks her spiritual awakening as he acts as a liaison between life on the surface and the world underground. Such symbolism has reached well past the novel, and we can find the White Rabbit represented in films (*The Matrix*), popular music ("White Rabbit" by Jefferson Airplane), and in video games. There was even a British undercover agent in World War II, Forest Yeo-Thomas, whose codename was "The White Rabbit." Meanwhile, the novel's other lagomorph character, the unpredictable yet philosophical March Hare, behaves as if it's always teatime.

Like the world of Carroll's imagination, not all is as it seems when it comes to the words we use to describe our crepuscular friends. A Belgian Hare is actually a rabbit, for instance, and a jackrabbit is really a hare. Descendants of a common ancestor, rabbits and hares are alike in some important ways. Both belong to the Lagomorpha order and the Leporidae family. They both have long ears and can gnaw through a vegetable garden faster than you can exclaim, "Oh no, not the kale!" But the similarities pretty much end there. For one thing, they are different species. Moreover, the hare's young, called leverets, are born in nests aboveground with their eyes open and largely independent, while rabbits give birth in underground burrows to kits who are completely reliant upon their mothers for the first few weeks of their lives. As adults, hares are larger than rabbits and could quite easily kick a rabbit's butt in a speed race.

But the language of lagomorphs goes much deeper than rabbit vs. hare. For a very long time—about 600 years, according to some etymologists—the word for rabbit in English was "coney," sometimes rendered as "cony" or "cunnie" but the first vowel was traditionally pronounced like the short *o* in "honey." We can see how this word relates to the way other European languages signify "rabbit," such as the Spanish *conejo*, the Catalan *conill*, the Italian *coniglio*, the Dutch *konijn*, the Swedish *kanin*, the Finnish *kani*, the German *Kaninchen*, the Old French *conil*, and the Manx Gaelic *coneeyn conning*. The Middle English *coney* is derived from the Latin *cuniculus*, which some historians maintain came from the Greek word for rabbit, *koniklos*, while others argue it came from Spain, to which rabbits are native. There is some evidence that "coney" to describe a rabbit could possibly be much older than six centuries; the word "conigrave," meaning "rabbit grove," appears in an English document known as the Marksbury charter purportedly dated 936 CE, though it might well be a thirteenth-century forgery.

"Coney" would have remained a popular appellation for rabbits were it not for the English fondness for slang. Beginning in the seventeenth century, Brits were using the word as a vulgar reference to women, so that by the 1800s, "coney" as a description for the animal was fully replaced by "rabbit." There was a wrinkle, however: the Christian Bible uses the word "coney" to indicate a hyrax, a rock-dwelling animal who looks marginally like a rabbit. Because the scripture was often read aloud in mixed company, and religious leaders didn't want people speaking or hearing a "dirty word" in a church, the revisionist powers that be declared that "coney" would henceforth be pronounced with a long *o*, to rhyme with "bony."

Presumably, everyone thus got through Bible readings with their modesty intact.

It has been suggested that New York's Coney Island was so named because it once had a large population of the animals hopping about (the old Dutch name was *Conyne Eylant* or "Rabbit Island"). Whether or not this is true, there are indisputably many locations in the world with monikers reflecting the tremendous influence of rabbits. This is especially the case in the British Isles, where you'll find such places as Coneyhurst in West Sussex, whose name means "wooded hill frequented by rabbits"; Conies Down, or "rabbit hill," in Lydford; Conisholme Cross, a crossroads in Fulstow that seems to mean "the rabbit meadow"; Conegar Hill in Broadwindsor, which refers to a "rabbit warren"; Coney Bury in Preshute, meaning "rabbit burrow"; the bucolically named Conies Dale in Peak Forest, which means "rabbit valley"; Knocknagoney (*cnoc na gCoiníní*) Down in Ireland, which is Gaelic for "hill of the rabbits," as well as Rabbit Island near the country's southwest shore; the Rabbit Islands off the north coast of Sutherland, Scotland; and of course a map full of Coney Lanes, Coney Hills, Coney Lodges, Coney Halls, and Rabbit Hills.

The word "coney" can be a little tricky in British place names, as it does not always refer to rabbits but sometimes to a word that the Vikings used for "king"; hence, Coneythorpe in North Yorkshire is derived from the Danish *Konig-thorpe*, meaning "king's farmstead." Likewise, Bunny, a village in the borough of Nottinghamshire, is not associated with a rabbit but is a compound of the Old English words *bune* and *eg* and means "reed-covered island." And don't expect to find any rabbits enjoying the sun and sand at Coney Beach in Wales—it is a small seaside amusement park named after Coney Island in New York.

What about the source of the word "rabbit"? In his 2008 academic tome *An Analytic Dictionary of English Etymology: An*

Introduction, linguistic scholar Anatoly Liberman addresses 55 words commonly dismissed as being of unknown origin and devotes nearly five densely packed pages to "rabbit," ultimately tracing it to about 1388. The word is all over the grammatical map, veering from the Flemish *robbe* to the Hebrew *rabah* (meaning "to multiply," something rabbits are undeniably accomplished at) to the Latin *rapidus* ("swift") to the Walloon *robett*, which was supposedly Anglicized to *rabet* so as not to be mistaken for the Middle English word for an Arabian horse, *rabite*—though it seems to me that in this case leaving the Walloon word alone would have been less confusing. In all fairness to Professor Liberman and his fellow scholars, this is just the tip of the carrot, and I won't test your patience by attempting to narrate all the semantic chiseling, shaping, sanding, and polishing that this word has been put through over the centuries to become what we now know as "rabbit." Suffice it to say it's a Germanic noun with a French suffix, and I think we'd all agree it's perfectly fine as it is and we should leave it alone.

Teasing out the precise provenance of "bun" is equally complicated. Many dictionaries and books on word origins from the nineteenth century tell the reader that "bun" (or some foreign derivation of it) describes either the tail end of a rabbit or some similar-looking form, such as a stump (as in a small, round cake, called a "bun") or a lump (as in "bunion"). Eliezer Edwards's 1882 compendium *Words, Facts, and Phrases* gets specific, defining "bun" as Scottish for "tail" and stating that "bunny" (sometimes spelled "bunnie") is a diminutive, meaning "little or short tail," and particularly applies to rabbits. The July–December 1860 issue of the scholarly journal *Notes and Queries* agrees with this, adding that an Old English word for the tail of a rabbit or hare is "scut," and this was often used to signify the animals themselves. (The word retains its historical meaning; you could either impress or confuse a veterinarian by mentioning it.)

Rabbit guardians often refer to these companion animals as "bunny," but that word began as a term of endearment for humans in the early seventeenth century. Its first recorded example is in a 1606 comedy called *Wily Beguiled* by an unknown author (the Elizabethan play probably existed at least a decade beforehand, but none of those early copies have survived). The character Will Cricket woos his beloved Peg Pudding with "... my love, my dove, my honey, my bunny, my duck, my dear, and my darling." By the late seventeenth century, according to the *Oxford Dictionary of Word Origins*, "bunny" was a pet name for rabbits, too, clearly as a derivation of "bun." In its more current form, "bunny" as a reference to women often has sexist connotations—think Playboy Bunny, beach bunny, and ski bunny, all of which reflect the sexual reputation of rabbits.

Leaping Lepus!

A few additional rabbit-related words to consider are lagomorph, Leporidae, Lepus, and leporine. The Greek word for hare is *lago*, and morph comes from *metamorphosis*, which is Greek for "transforming." So, lagomorph means "hare shaped" and scientifically refers to any members of the mammalian order comprised of rabbits, hares, and pikas, the latter of whom resemble guinea pigs and cannot leap like rabbits and hares. Unless you happen to be at high altitude in the mountains of Asia or North America, you're unlikely to ever see a pika. Rabbits and hares belong to the biological family Leporidae, which is Latin meaning "those that resemble Lepus (hare)." Finally, the adjective leporine is another Latin word linked to Lepus, as it relates to animals who are hare-like. In the same way that feline refers to cats and ursine refers to bears, leporine means rabbits and hares. File these under *M* for minutiae, which is Latin for trifle.

If it were up to Albert E. Wood, you'd be hearing the word bunny a lot more these days. In 1957, Dr. Wood, an eminent professor of biology at Amherst College in Massachusetts, produced a paper he titled "What, If Anything, Is a Rabbit?" in which he explained why rabbits are no longer classified as rodents but as lagomorphs. He also proposed referring to a rabbit as a "bunny" instead of a "rabbit" since so many people mistakenly call these animals a "hare." That Dr. Wood's suggestion never really caught on probably has more to do with the public's reluctance to read obscure academic journals than with their vocabulary preferences.

While we're on the subject of "rabbit," there are those who invoke the word as a kind of prayer. According to a popular superstition, saying "rabbit" upon waking on the first day of the month brings the utterer good luck. In the reasonable expectation that doing a good thing twice will double your fortune, some say "rabbit, rabbit," while still other hopeful petitioners place their bets on the winning formula of "rabbit, rabbit, rabbit." This magical phrase seems to have started in England, where it was recorded in *Notes and Queries* in 1909. A contributor writes: "My two daughters are in the habit of saying 'Rabbits!' on the first day of each month. The word must be spoken aloud, and be the first word said in the month. It brings luck for that month." Another parent adds: "My little daughter has for some time been in the habit of saying 'Rabbit' on the first day of each month. The word to be most efficacious must be spoken up the chimney, and be the first word said in the month. I am told that if this is done the performer will receive a present." Still another variation is to say "white rabbit" or "white rabbits."

Adults are just as likely to summon rabbits for help, of course. Indeed, according to an article in a 1935 edition of a British newspaper, "Even Mr. [Franklin] Roosevelt, the President of the United States, has confessed to a friend that he says 'Rabbits' on the first of every month—and, what is more, he would not think of omitting the utterance on any account." (Perhaps this is what inspired FDR's daughter Anna to write her two 1934 books *Scamper: The Bunny Who Went to the White House*, about the adventures of a rabbit who comes to live with the president's grandchildren, and its sequel *Scamper's Christmas: More About the White House Bunny*.) And as a young girl, comedian Gilda Radner is said to have used the words "bunny, bunny" to protect her from bad dreams—a practice that morphed into saying it for good luck on the first day of every month as she got older.

Folk wisdom aside, much of what we know about European rabbits today is credited to the work of Welsh naturalist Ronald Lockley. In 1955, Lockley embarked on a four-year study of rabbit behavior for the British Nature Conservancy. To accomplish his task, he created an artificial warren with an enormous glass window and observation hut on one side beneath a large meadow on his 260-acre (105-hectare) estate in Pembrokeshire, Wales. Day and night, in all kinds of weather, Lockley observed the rabbits' lives in the tunnels and rooms: their intricate community, their relationships, their daily struggles. He published his findings in the November 1961 edition of the *Journal of Animal Ecology* but soon expanded them, and the resulting book, *The Private Life of the Rabbit*, was published in 1964. It was a groundbreaking work of controlled observation, and *The New York Times Literary Supplement* said Lockley's book "shows the rabbit to be a more complex fellow than one had thought."

Among the many fans of *The Private Life of the Rabbit* was an English civil servant named Richard Adams, who in his spare time was writing a fantasy tale to entertain his daughters. He used Lockley's meticulous account of rabbit life as the basis for what would become his 1972 novel *Watership Down*. Set in south-central England, the story focuses on a band of brave rabbits and their quest to relocate their colony. The characters communicate primarily in English, but when referring to their mythology and the objects in their world they often revert to Lapine, a language Adams invented for the book (and clearly named after *lapin*, the French word for rabbit). Lapine is used to create an environment beyond human experience, serving to deanthropomorphize the rabbit characters; Adams not only gives them their own language, but he also never has them do anything a real rabbit couldn't do. The rabbits of *Watership Down* have meaningful relationships, rich inner lives, and important cultural practices, and their unique language helps establish this.

With a vocabulary that includes *hrair* (meaning "a lot"), *thlay* ("fur"), *hrududu* (a "machine," like a tractor or car), and *narn* ("nice" or "pleasant"), Lapine has been described by various linguists as being reminiscent of Arabic, Irish, Scottish Gaelic, and Welsh. (In his 2006 *Encyclopedia of Fictional and Fantastic Languages*, Stephen Cain suggests that Adams studied Arabic during his military service in Palestine.) Adams has explained that he wanted Lapine to have a "wuffy, fluffy" quality—what we might imagine a talking rabbit would sound like. Lapine has no grammar, however; it is simply a collection of nouns, adjectives, and verbs. To further emphasize that Lapine is different, Adams gives the nouns the plural suffix *il*, rather than the English *s*. Two or more cars, for example, would be *hrududil*.

Adams acts as an interpreter, carefully transcribing Lapine dialogue into English. He provides definitions of Lapine words throughout early chapters (and a complete glossary), but he trusts that as readers move through the narrative, they will learn enough of the rabbits' language to recognize most of the important words and phrases. By the time the character Bigwig boldly shouts "Silflay hraka," we do not need any translation to understand that he is inviting his adversary to eat shit.

Over the decades, many readers have construed *Watership Down* as some sort of allegory—like George Orwell's *Animal Farm*—but Adams's daughters, Juliet and Rosamond, insist their father never intended the novel to be more than what it was: "It's just a story about rabbits," he told them. To ensure the book was as true to the lives of real rabbits as possible, Adams asked Ronald Lockley to read a final draft. The scientist "contributed several good suggestions," Adams noted in his introduction. "I remember, in particular, that he devised the passage in *Watership Down* in which the rabbits raid Nuthanger Farm" and release several bunnies being held in hutches. There is a real Watership Down, by the way (a "down" is a hill). You'll find it near the English village of Kingsclere, in Hampshire. And, yes, it is home to rabbit warrens, though not as many as in Adams's day.

Watership Down is one example of the genre known as wild-animal fiction, and its genesis can be traced to the turn of the twentieth century, when writers such as Jack London, Charles G. D. Roberts, and Mabel Osgood Wright took a more realistic approach to portraying animals in literature. Among the other pioneers of this genre is the Canadian storyteller and wildlife artist Ernest Thompson Seton, whose 1898 bestseller *Wild Animals I Have Known* includes the short story of a young cottontail rabbit named Raggylug, or simply Rag. As the title suggests, Seton presents his narrative as a collection of factual accounts, emphatically informing the reader: "These stories are true. Although I have left the strict line of historical truth in many places, the animals in this book were all real characters. They lived the lives I have depicted, and showed the stamp of heroism and personality more strongly by far than it has been in the power of my pen to tell."

Seton takes great care to describe how rabbits communicate with one another, noting that "rabbits have no speech as we understand it, but they have a way of conveying ideas by a system of sounds, signs, scents, whisker-touches, movements, and example that answers the purpose of speech." He explains that he will translate the rabbit language into English (much like Adams does) and reminds the reader that he has invented nothing. After this preamble, Seton commences a credible look at the life of Rag and his mother, Molly, who lived together in a nest beneath the tall grass of a forest near a marshy pond. The author tells us that he was personally acquainted with these rabbits, and so it is as an informed observer that he is able to accurately depict their lives and the perils they faced. When he quotes Molly speaking to Rag, we are asked to accept her dialogue as a faithful presentation of her thoughts.

Molly keeps Rag safe and imparts to him such important lessons as how to communicate over long distances. "As soon as Rag was big enough to go out alone, his mother taught him the signal code," Seton writes. "Rabbits telegraph each other by thumping the ground with their hind feet. Along the ground sound carries far; a thump that at six feet from the earth is not heard at twenty yards will, near the ground, be heard at least one hundred yards." He explains that a single thump means "look out" or "freeze," two slow thumps mean "come," two fast thumps mean "danger," and three very fast thumps mean "run for dear life."

Some scientifically minded detractors assailed Seton's writing and labeled him a "nature faker" for purporting to understand the inner lives of animals, such as how they express themselves. Seton, they argued, had no business using poetic license in "Raggylug, the Story of a Cottontail Rabbit" and other tales—or at least he should have acknowledged that he was blending fiction with fact rather than claim that he was privy to the thoughts and feelings of rabbits and other animals. In a screed for the March 1903 issue of *Atlantic Monthly* magazine, nature essayist John Burroughs evokes surprise that Seton is able to discern the secrets of rabbits, foxes, horses, etc., when such a hyper-observant naturalist as Henry David Thoreau failed to do so. Burroughs writes, "There are no stories of animal intelligence and cunning on record, that I am aware of, that match his." He didn't mean that as a compliment.

Seton was undoubtedly ahead of his time in believing that nonhuman animals possess not only thoughts and feelings but also the ability to reason and pass survival skills along to their young. Although critics targeted other wild-animal writers and their improbable depictions, including Jack London and William J. Long, Seton felt particularly attacked, and he responded to the nature faker controversy by backing away from animal stories and instead publishing scientific studies of wildlife. Long, on the other hand, took a different approach. In 1905, he penned a series of essays in *Harper's Magazine* under the pseudonym Peter Rabbit that explored, from the perspective of the "author," animal intelligence and the human condition.

By 1905, Peter Rabbit was practically a household name, thanks to another nature artist with a flair for storytelling. Helen Beatrix Potter (1866–1943) first found her way into the literary world in 1890, when several of her drawings of her rabbit Benjamin Bouncer were used in a book of verse titled *A Happy Pair* by Frederic Weatherly, who would go on to write the lyrics for the Irish ballad "Danny Boy." In 1900, Beatrix (she went by her middle name to distinguish her from her mother, also named Helen) used a letter she had written to the son of her former governess as the foundation of her first picture book, *The Tale of Peter Rabbit*, which she wrote and illustrated and which was commercially published in 1902, amid the golden age of children's literature in Europe and the United States. In England, after the death of Queen Victoria the year before, the Victorian era and its conservative code of conduct gave way to the queen's son and heir, Edward VII, and the more relaxed standards of the Edwardian era. This period is regarded as one of enormous social advances. Declining in popularity were the tight-fitting corsets of the 1800s, for instance—women could now presumably take a deep breath in their undergarments without risking a fractured rib, though their best chance for independence and a home away from their parents still lay in marriage.

For Beatrix Potter, the path to an independent life turned out to be a direct route between her talents with a paintbrush and her way with words. Published when Beatrix was 36 years old, *Peter Rabbit* gave her much of the freedom she had longed for, and in the autumn of 1905 she purchased a 34-acre (14-hectare) farm known as Hill Top in England's Lake District. Although Beatrix would live with her strict mother and father in London until 1913, Hill Top was her personal retreat, and here amid the rugged beauty of the countryside she found inspiration for many of her later children's stories, including *The Tale of Tom Kitten*, *The Tale of Jemima Puddle-Duck*, and *The Roly-Poly Pudding*.

But it is for *Peter Rabbit* that she is best remembered. The story invites us into the world of "four little rabbits"—the obedient sisters Flopsy, Mopsy, and Cottontail, and their brother, the mischievous Peter—as well as their mother, who enjoys cooking and believes no problem exists that can't be solved with a cup of tea. They all live in a comfortable burrow beneath a large fir tree, nicely appointed with a fireplace and an impressive assortment of crockery. For her tale, Beatrix carefully considered not only the meaning of words and how they sound but also their arrangement on the page. Observe, for example, how she introduces the reader to the rabbit siblings in the book's early editions, with the names Flopsy, Mopsy, Cottontail, and Peter each appearing on their own line, like the descending steps of a staircase, in order to emphasize them individually. Or appreciate how she uses lively illustrations to help young readers understand and contextualize words that they might be unfamiliar with, like "sieve," "gooseberry net," and "cucumber frame."

Childhood Muse

The earliest literary endeavors by Beatrix Potter and Richard Adams were of course centered on rabbits, but another well-known writer perhaps not famous for his leporine prose found inspiration in bunnies. The first story ever written by the prolific horror master Stephen King featured a large white bunny named Mr. Rabbit Trick who drove his animal friends around town in a car. King was about six years old. He wrote four more stories about Mr. Rabbit Trick, and his mother was so impressed that she paid him 25 cents for each one. King recalls in his memoir *On Writing*: "Four stories. A quarter apiece. That was the first buck I made in this business." Mr. Rabbit Trick would make a cameo appearance in the author's 2020 novella *If It Bleeds* as someone's beloved stuffed bunny.

Indeed, as important to the narrative as the text is the artwork, which the author painted herself and from the very beginning makes it apparent that this is a subversive tale. Mrs. Rabbit tells the wee rabbits that they can play in the field or down the lane, but she cautions them to stay out of Mr. McGregor's garden. Although the sisters are clearly listening attentively to Mum's warning, Peter is illustrated with his back to her, and the defiant look on his face tells us that he has no intention of keeping clear of old McGregor's property. Soon Flopsy, Mopsy, and Cottontail are off picking blackberries, and Peter is heading straight for the forbidden vegetable patch, where his skills as a trickster will quickly come into play. In Peter's world, as in real life, actions have consequences, and his love of adventure leads him into trouble not terribly unlike what a naughty human child might experience (that is, minus hiding in a watering can or being assisted by talking sparrows). In the end, the self-indulgent young bunny's mischief earns him little more than the stink eye from his dutiful sisters.

Publication of *Peter Rabbit* began in October 1902 with a run of 8000 copies and then subsequent runs of 12,000 in November and 8220 in December. By November of the following year, the publisher was busy preparing a sixth printing. "The public must be fond of rabbits!" wrote an astonished Beatrix, who had privately printed 250 copies of the book in 1901 for family and friends after initially being rejected by several publishers. Incidentally, she was as clever as she was talented, and she presaged the era of product merchandising by designing and patenting both a Peter Rabbit doll in 1903 and then, the next year, a Peter Rabbit board game ("Intensely Amusing," proclaims a game box from the 1930s). We will explore her rabbit paintings in Chapter Five.

Beatrix Potter's publisher, Frederick Warne & Co., was thrilled with the success they had on their hands; indeed, Peter Rabbit would become their bestselling property. But in their glee they made a colossal blunder: they neglected to properly secure copyright protection for *The Tale of Peter Rabbit* in the United States, an enormous market where unscrupulous book publishers were quick to mine profits from the literary rabbit by releasing unauthorized versions of the text and artwork. Plagiarized copies of the book began appearing within two years, and the results were both a financial and emotional blow to Beatrix. Some books feature her text but someone else's illustrations. Other books consist of her illustrations but another writer's text. Still others contain pictures and a story that bear only a passing resemblance to what she had created.

Not all interpretations of Peter Rabbit beyond those approved by Frederick Warne & Co. are necessarily pirated, however. Because copyrights and trademarks can either lapse or expire, creative materials that were previously protected can suddenly become part of the public domain, giving anyone permission to use them. The understanding of what is covered by copyright and what is in the public domain can sometimes be as muddy as Farmer McGregor's garden. What is clear is that Beatrix Potter's work has inspired countless creations having no connection with her other than the name Peter Rabbit. In her book *The Case of Peter Rabbit*, Margaret Mackey catalogs a wide variety of such products in the USA, Canada, and Great Britain, including not only books but also a children's film that casts Peter Rabbit as a Christian preacher, singing songs about Jesus and dancing with animated vegetables. (We can only imagine what Beatrix Potter—who wrote "All outward forms of religion are almost useless, and are the causes of endless strife"—would think of that.) Another cartoon, writes Dr. Mackey, "alters just about every essential aspect of the original story. Peter is given a set of buck teeth, an American accent, a fourth sister Hopsy, an entirely changed character, a large set of allies, comical sidekicks and enemies, and an entirely new plot."

The Rabbit Scribe

Sometimes, rabbits do the writing themselves—or at least they are depicted doing so. On display at the Princeton University Art Museum is a small ceramic vase dating to 670–750 CE that was used by the Maya as a drinking cup (probably for chocolate). Painted on the vase is a detailed palace scene, where a deity associated with trade, shamanism, and war (currently known as god L until his name has been deciphered) sits on his throne and fastens a bracelet onto the wrist of a young woman. Off to the side two men are about to separate the head of a sacrificial victim from his shoulders. Seated on the floor to the left of the god, near the throne, is a rabbit who is using a quill or paintbrush to write in a book. Whether the rabbit is dutifully recording events, composing poetry, spying, or writing something else remains unknown.

In an example of how influential *Peter Rabbit* was, when conservationist and journalist Thornton Burgess of Massachusetts read it to his son shortly after the book's publication, the boy became so fixated on the story that ever after any rabbit had to be named Peter. When Burgess penned his own children's stories that would eventually be published in the 1910 book *Old Mother West Wind*, he obligingly named the rabbit protagonist Peter Rabbit. He always identified Beatrix Potter as the originator of the name, even if she wasn't entirely thrilled by his acknowledgement. Burgess's books enjoyed enough success to merit a musical adaptation, *Peter Rabbit in Dreamland*, which ran on three different New York stages in 1915 and 1916.

Much less known today is *Rabbit Hill*, written and illustrated by Robert Lawson, who created a number of animal-themed novels for pre-teens during the first half of the twentieth century. (He was also famous for having illustrated *The Story of Ferdinand*, a children's book about a bull who would rather sniff flowers than participate in bullfights, which seems perfectly reasonable to me.) At the heart of the narrative is Little Georgie, son of Mother and Father Rabbit, who is excited to tell his parents that the Big House on the hill will soon be occupied. The rabbits and other animals who call Rabbit Hill home are anxious because the house has been vacant for years and its previous tenants had neglected the garden, leaving no food for the small animals. Everyone wonders what the New Folks will be like. Will they be planting folk who will revive the fallow garden and lawn and treat the animals with kindness? "This news of Georgie's may promise the approach of a more felicitous and bountiful era," says Father, who is even more articulate and optimistic than most college graduates.

The rabbits not only speak and read English, but they also walk upright, cook meals, and use imperial measurements to calculate distances. Notwithstanding these nods to the human world, they are clearly lagomorphs, as evidenced by the framed portraits of produce that hang neatly in their burrow. To everyone's relief, the new homeowners turn out to be good people. Father Rabbit tests their benevolence by running in front of their car, which the driver stops quickly. The next day the humans put up a sign on the road reading, "Please drive carefully on account of small animals." They're also enthusiastic gardeners who generously share their bounty with all the animals. There is enough for everyone, the tale seems to say, and it ends with the good folks placing in the garden a statue of St. Francis, patron saint of animals, whom all the critters somehow recognize.

Lawson wrote *Rabbit Hill* during the waning days of World War II, and it's tempting to view his fable as a parable reflecting the peace and prosperity people longed for. That may be, but he began the book at the prompting of his editor, May Massee, who suggested that he create a story based on the rabbits living near his Westport, Connecticut, home—a large house that he and his wife, Marie, built in 1936 and named "Rabbit Hill." The couple are clearly the "New Folks" of the novel, and in real life too they enjoyed a special kinship with their subterranean neighbors. Lawson recalled that the rabbits seemed to magically appear whenever he received good news about the book. A small rabbit hopped over to the mailbox the afternoon Massee's letter arrived telling him how much she had enjoyed reading it. Another bunny showed up when the beautiful proofs of the illustrations were delivered. More rabbits emerged on the day his book was chosen as a Junior Library Guild title and, later, when he received positive reviews and royalty checks. "I don't know what good it did them," he said, "but they came to tell us about it anyway."

Lawson hadn't seen any rabbits on the property for a long while when a bunny resembling the book's main protagonist appeared at the house and spent ten minutes looking through the window. The author confidently told Marie, "Well, there's Little Georgie with some good news about *Rabbit Hill*." The very next day, he received a letter from Frances Clarke Sayers of the 1945 Newbery Medal Selection Committee informing him that *Rabbit Hill* had been chosen for the prestigious award, which is given for the most distinguished contribution to children's literature in the USA. Lawson later joked that he wasn't superstitious, but he was a little worried because the book he'd just finished was about an elephant.

Upon accepting the Newbery prize, Lawson credited Marie and his editor for their help with *Rabbit Hill* but also hinted that he might have been channeling the rabbits themselves. "I pushed the pencil and pecked at the typewriter," he said, "but someone else certainly must have written it. With every other book I've ever done I have always made a complete outline and had everything planned up to the last line, but for this one I had nothing at all. I hadn't the faintest idea of what it was going to be or how it was to come out. In fact it started to be something completely different, but once it was begun someone took hold of it and it just went ahead and wrote itself." It was a good season for rabbits, he added, because *Harvey*, the play about an invisible bunny, had won the Pulitzer and Little Georgie took home the Newbery.

Another tale not well known today is "Prince Rabbit" by A. A. Milne, famous for his stories featuring Winnie-the-Pooh and friends. Published in 1924, two years before the first Pooh book, "Prince Rabbit" is a humorous fairytale featuring a lagomorph who bears little resemblance to Rabbit from Milne's more popular work, in which the character is a bit bossy and self-important. Whereas Rabbit's plans don't always have the intended result, Prince Rabbit is quite a clever fellow, and he enters a competition to be named successor to a king who has no heir. He participates in sword fighting (to prove his strength), riddle-solving and arithmetic (to prove his intelligence), and standing (to demonstrate he can remain upright on two legs for royal speeches). In each instance he plays the role of the trickster and finally enlists the aid of an old enchanter, which is a rather subtle twist on the magician's rabbit trope.

Rabbit Hill, The Tale of Peter Rabbit, "Raggylug," *Watership Down, The Private Life of the Rabbit,* and "Prince Rabbit" all appeared in the wake of *Snowdrop: Or the Adventures of a White Rabbit,* which was published in English in 1873 as an autobiography. The front cover reads "Related by himself," though the memoir is actually by a woman named Mathilde Sandras, who wrote it in 1869 under the French title *Mémoires d'un Lapin Blanc* ("Memoirs of a White Rabbit"), in which Snowdrop is called Jeannot. Animal autobiographies were a popular genre in the nineteenth century, and they were often a thinly veiled effort to nurture compassion for animals in young readers. Snowdrop is a white, dark-eyed rabbit who is born and raised in a young ladies' boarding school in France, where is he kept primarily in an outdoor hutch, even in winter, and is often neglected. He shivers in the cold and is threatened by predators. He complains of depression and lack of food, though he is generally much loved and admired. Snowdrop does not have the ability to speak, but he does have a philosophical mind, and this is especially clear when he's expressing his thoughts about the importance of kindness. "Good deeds are worth more than good thoughts," he writes, and, "It is very cruel to amuse oneself at the expense of the weak." Such is Snowdrop's depth of compassion that he even finds it lamentable that some species prey on others, asking, "Why cannot each animal be content, as we rabbits are, with the grass of the field?"

Snowdrop was published in England four years before Anna Sewell's horse-themed book *Black Beauty,* which is widely considered the beginning of children's narratives focused on animal welfare. Both titles are presented as first-person memoirs, but while *Black Beauty* was a bestseller, *Snowdrop* has been all but forgotten. I am not suggesting that Sandras has written the better book (its plot is weaker), but it deserves a more prominent place within animal literature, especially among stories that encourage treating animals with kindness.

With personalities and behavior that suggest both strength and transience, rabbits have inspired poets, too. Much of the poetry that you'll find devoted to rabbits (and hares) dwells on their status as prey animals in some way, but there are poets who have found unique approaches to celebrate these animals in verse. In "A Rabbit as King of the Ghosts" by Wallace Stevens, a rabbit watches a cat before rising into the sky (or so it seems). The poem has been widely interpreted since its publication in 1937. Some have analyzed it as a comic parable about the dangers of hubris, while others propose that Stevens was imagining what it feels like to *be* a rabbit. (The poet may have had a particular sympathy for rabbits. In a letter to one of his publishers a few months before the poem appeared in print, Stevens wrote that a rabbit could be seen outside the window of his home in Hartford, Connecticut, and that he took a keen interest in watching him each morning. "I spend the time worrying about the rabbit and wondering what particular thing he is having for breakfast.")

I am especially fond of "Song of the Rabbits Outside the Tavern" by Elizabeth Coatsworth, as excerpted in this book's epigraph. Published in 1934, Coatsworth's three-stanza poem captures the perspective of wild rabbits who are comparing their lives with those of humans inside a rural pub. Peeking through a window, they observe the humans warming themselves with "suns they have in a cave" (a fireplace) and remark on the "stars each on a tall white stem" (candles), but note that "they never dance as we dance." They even look disapprovingly on the dog and cat who lie inside by the fire. The rabbits may not have all these comforts, they conclude, but they're able to play beneath the pines and dance under a winter's moon.

The sonnet "Hares at Play" by John Clare narrates the nocturnal activities of hares who frolic carefree after "the birds are gone to bed and the cows are still." Like other Clare poems that epitomize the essence of country life, "Hares at Play" offers a glimpse of nature; in this case, it's the quick movement of hares who are all too aware that they have a limited time in which to indulge their desire to "dance and play" and "lick the dew-fall from the barley's beard." As a new day dawns, they retreat "quick as fear" back to their hidden lair.

Because rabbits and hares have a fundamental place in literature, history, and mythology, they figure prominently in common idioms. To "go down the rabbit hole," for instance, is to enter an especially strange or difficult situation and is likely an allusion to Lewis Carroll's *Alice's Adventures in Wonderland,* in which the title character falls down a rabbit hole and ends up in an eccentric world. A "rabbit punch," which was used by boxers but is now illegal in the sport, is a blow to the base of the skull or back of the neck. The golfing world has its own "rabbit," used to refer either to a professional player who must qualify for a tournament or to a game played among three or four golfers, as does cricket, where a "rabbit" is a very poor batsman. To say two people were "at it like rabbits" refers to them copulating, which could lead to someone saying "the rabbit died," an archaic expression meaning a woman is pregnant. This latter idiom comes from a 1930s test in which the urine of a woman who suspected she might be in a family way (another archaic expression) was injected into a rabbit. "Harebrained" has been around since 1548, according to the *Oxford English Dictionary,* and describes a foolish or reckless idea or act, which is rather ironic considering that many cultures portray hares and rabbits as tricksters and thus possessing above-average intelligence. To "buy the rabbit" is to fare badly or come off worse in a situation.

Someone who is as "mad as a March hare" behaves irrationally or unpredictably. As mentioned in the chapter on Easter, this phrase finds its origin in the excitable manner of European hares, who are said to act impulsively during their mating season, which peaks in March. The idiom is centuries old but was personified by the March Hare character from Carroll's novel. And that leads me to "rabbit trail" or "bunny trailing," which describes a story that goes off on a tangent.

That so much of our language is related to lagomorphs says as much about our fascination with rabbits and hares as it does about the way we communicate. When we can use a rabbit-themed phrase—good or bad—as a linguistic shortcut, for instance, we are in a way acknowledging the central role these animals play in our culture, where their behavior and position are so familiar that nearly everyone recognizes what the expression means. Of course, rabbits themselves do have a language of their own, and we'll explore this in Chapter Eight.

Chapter Five

Rabbits in Art

Rabbits speak to me in spirit. They are very pleased that I am painting them.
—Hunt Slonem

It took just ten minutes for a New York art collector with very deep pockets to make history. In May of 2019, Robert Mnuchin bid furiously against four other prospective buyers at Christie's auction house to win *Rabbit*—a steel rabbit sculpture three and a half feet high (about 105 cm)—for US$92 million and change. As this book goes to print, that represents the most anyone has paid for a work by a living artist. That artist, Jeff Koons, created *Rabbit* in 1986, and his reflective cast of an inflatable plastic toy is considered one of the most iconic works of twentieth-century art and a symbol of '80s excess.

As a piece of art, *Rabbit* may not be to everyone's taste. It looks like nothing more than a child's silver balloon animal; indeed, a 54-foot (16-m) inflatable reproduction of the sculpture floated through Midtown Manhattan as part of Macy's Thanksgiving Day Parade in 2007. But many art lovers see something else. Of his first encounter with the work, art historian Kirk Varnedoe, who would become the chief curator of painting and sculpture at the Museum of Modern Art in New York, wrote, "It seemed to me instantly, by involuntary reflex—and still does by long reflection—that this bunny is one of those very rare hits at the exact center of the target." Artnet News called the work "the holy grail of Koons works among certain collecting circles" and noted that Christie's had given *Rabbit* an extraordinary pre-sale display, with the sculpture perched on a pedestal in a custom-built room. Perhaps the auction house said it best in their essay for the sale, observing that the work "taps into the visual language of childhood, of all that is pure and innocent."

The rabbit as a symbol of childhood innocence is of course one of the powerful aspects of their appeal as an artistic subject. Even in religious iconography and artworks, where rabbits are frequently associated with rebirth and resurrection, their presence is often used to invoke the theme of chastity. This seems rather at odds with the tradition of celebrating rabbits for their fertility, though a medieval belief that hares and, by association, rabbits were hermaphrodites who could reproduce without copulating no doubt gave painters of religious scenes a reason to include them. Arguably the most famous example is an oil painting by the Renaissance master Titian that has come to be known as *Madonna of the Rabbit* or *Madonna and Child with St. Catherine*. Currently on display at the Louvre in Paris, *Madonna of the Rabbit* was painted sometime between 1525 and 1530 and depicts an outdoor scene of St. Catherine handing the baby Jesus to Mary, who is using one hand to pet (or perhaps carefully restrain) a small white rabbit seated on her cloak. Behind Mary and to her left is a shepherd, whom some experts identify as her husband, Joseph. The tableau is brimming with Christian imagery—the use of white to symbolize Mary's purity, for instance, and the myth of rabbits producing offspring asexually echoes the story of a virgin birth— but one can't help notice that the infant is clearly focused on the rabbit, who is returning Jesus' gaze and remains alert, ears up. (I can certainly understand the rabbit's apprehension; I would never trust a toddler with a bunny, no matter who their parents were.)

Two rabbits make an appearance in Hans Baldung Grien's 1511 woodcut *The Fall of Mankind*, sometimes referred to as *Adam and*

Eve. The scene is the Garden of Eden, and the biblical serpent is coiled around the Tree of Knowledge as Eve holds the forbidden fruit. With his left hand on Eve's bosom, Adam seems to have other temptations on his mind, and this is perhaps emphasized by the rabbits behind them.

Likewise, Hieronymus Bosch's intricate triptych oil painting *The Garden of Earthly Delights*, completed in about 1500, features brown rabbits near Adam and Eve on the left panel. In typical Bosch fashion, however, the center panel includes a rabbit on the back of a fish and another on the beak of a bird. Things get progressively stranger as we look to the right and find a depiction of hell that is dark and disturbing (though, to be fair, it could hardly be otherwise); here a very large rabbit, or possibly a hare, blows a hunter's horn and carries a bleeding woman strung up on a pole by her feet. Yet in a painting that also incorporates three-headed birds, a pig dressed in a nun's habit, and flowers blossoming from someone's buttocks, a rabbit killing humans seems downright conventional by comparison.

Perhaps a more universal example of lagomorph symbolism is the three-rabbits (or three-hares) icon, a circular motif that has been found at sacred sites in a number of countries. The rabbit trio share a total of three ears, yet through an optical illusion, it appears each running animal has two. Although seen on medieval churches in Europe and thought by some to represent the Holy Trinity, the image dates much earlier in China, where it was prominently painted onto the ceilings of Buddhist temples in the sixth century. Indeed, the three rabbits are a common Buddhist image, found within monasteries in Tibet and Ladakh, where one can see four-rabbit symbols, as well. An Islamic reliquary casket made in the thirteenth century features the three rabbits on its base. The emblem also appears in a Jewish manuscript from 1309 and on Jewish gravestones in Ukraine. And as if all that weren't enough, the triple hares can be found on an eleventh-century

Hindu medallion. The county of Devon in England seems to be something of a hot spot for the icon, which can be seen on the ceilings of at least 17 churches there (the search continues for more).

Fittingly, a trio of experts in different fields has been researching the three-hares motif at sites around the world. Art historian Sue Andrew, photographer Chris Chapman, and archeologist Tom Greeves created the Three Hares Project in 2000 to document and attempt to unlock the mystery of one of the world's most baffling symbols. "I feel that the reason that the motif appears in so many cultures is that it is so deeply satisfying on many levels," says Dr. Andrew, noting that the hare is a mysterious creature often associated with magic. Because some medieval Christian and Islamic sources claimed that the hare was capable of procreating on their own, she says, many people believed that the icon had the power to ward off evil or bad luck. "For example, on Islamic metalwork, it often sits alongside inscriptions invoking happiness and blessings to the owner." In one medieval Christian context, meanwhile, the hares appear as part of an historiated initial depicting the first temptation of Christ. "Wrapped in the tail of a wyvern, a two-legged dragon, which passes stones to a devil, the hares here may represent a lack of firmness in faith, or a testing of faith, which could lead to succumbing to temptation—hares could be associated with both lust and virginity as a result of their hermaphroditism."

The design's rotational symmetry also creates a visually arresting pattern that Dr. Andrew believes probably appealed to many cultures. "Each must have appreciated its puzzle aspect," she says. And not lost on her is how the doubling of the ears reflects a hare's (and rabbit's) practice of doubling back and forth when they are pursued—a survival habit we will explore in Chapter Eight.

A more recent rabbit-themed optical illusion was created by an anonymous illustrator and published in a German humor magazine in 1892. Known simply as the duck–rabbit image (or sometimes the rabbit–duck illusion), it is a black-and-white sketch that may be interpreted as either the head of a rabbit facing right or the head of a duck facing left. They share a common eye, but the rabbit's ears can also be seen as the duck's bill, opened slightly. A month after its German debut it appeared in the US publication *Harper's Weekly*, but the drawing's fame was sealed seven years later when psychologist Joseph Jastrow began using it to determine how rapidly someone can see the second animal and how quickly they could switch between the two. His research suggested that perception is not only what a person sees but is also a mental activity—in other words, we see with the mind as well as the eye. (You have a creative and efficient brain, Dr. Jastrow concluded, if your mind can easily alternate the rabbit and duck images.)

The drawing has since been recreated many times for various purposes. Among the cleverest is a cartoon by Paul Noth for a 2014 issue of *The New Yorker* magazine. In the single panel, two medieval-looking armies are lined up in a field for battle, facing each other, and each displaying flags and banners with the identical rabbit–duck icon. With his sword raised, a soldier in one of the armies rallies his confederates with the cry, "There can be no peace until they renounce their Rabbit God and accept our Duck God!" I will let you decide what Noth is trying to say about religion, but I appreciate that the artist has returned the image to its original intent: as a source of humor.

Interestingly, in a 1993 study, when the duck–rabbit image was shown to 265 children and adults on an Easter Sunday, most saw a rabbit; when it was shown to 276 people in October, most saw a duck.

Because rabbits and hares are also linked to fertility, sexuality, and love, they appear in secular art, as well. Among the earliest examples is a small still-life fresco found in a home in Pompeii,

Italy, an ancient Roman city that was destroyed by volcanic gases and debris after the eruption of Mount Vesuvius in 79 CE. The remarkably preserved fresco, now at the Naples National Archaeological Museum, depicts a large rabbit beside four figs. Rabbits and hares were a common theme in the classical world, where paintings and mosaics of these animals adorned houses and public spaces.

A much more recognized lagomorph painting is known in English as *Young Hare*, a watercolor-and-gouache portrait by Albrecht Dürer. (The original German title, *Feldhase*—or "Field Hare"—is more accurate, since the hare is clearly mature.) In this 1502 nature study, Dürer renders a hare with nearly photorealistic detail; indeed, some have suggested that the hare must have lived in Dürer's studio for the artist to have achieved such realism. The shades of brown, the softly mottled fur, the delicate whiskers, and the golden light create a portrait that is both warm and dramatic. Not surprisingly, *Young Hare* has pride of place in Vienna's Albertina Museum, where it has become the city's unofficial mascot. What *is* surprising is that it remains mostly in hiding. "An artwork as precious and irreplaceable as Dürer's *Hare*, which suffers most from light, can only be exhibited very rarely and for a very short time," says Christof Metzger, the museum's chief curator. After about three months of public display, the fragile masterpiece requires a number of years in dark storage amid a humidity level of less than 50 percent for the paper to adequately rest. "Since 1900, he has only been publicly presented eight times," Metzger says.

What makes *Young Hare* especially significant is that Dürer was working at a time when painting animals by themselves was largely frowned upon; they were not thought to be worthy of artistic consideration, and this view wouldn't change for two centuries. Challenging this attitude, Dürer created not only an evocative likeness of a hare but also an influential painting that has inspired countless works by other artists, including *A Hare in*

the Forest by Hans Hoffman (1585) and a faithfully reproduced —
albeit bright pink and oversized — sculpture of a hare by Ottmar
Hörl displayed outside the Vienna State Opera.

More in line with the prevailing opinion of animals in fine art
at the time is Piero di Cosimo's *Venus, Mars, and Cupid* (1505),
which features the Roman goddess of love and beauty and the god
of war reclining postcoital and nearly naked in a meadow with
their infant son, Cupid, who has a gray-white rabbit practically
nibbling his fingertips. The rabbit, half of whom is hidden behind
Venus, here represents sexuality. The scene is not taken from
classical mythology but recounts a liaison mentioned by Homer
in *The Odyssey* and Ovid in *The Metamorphosis* and functions as
an allegory of the conquest of love over war. As with Titian's
painting, we see here how artists link children and rabbits.

They also link rabbits with themes of fertility and spring, as
in Francesco del Cossa's 1470 fresco *Allegory of April: Triumph of
Venus*. In ancient Rome, the month of April was marked with a
festival in honor of Venus, and animals regarded as highly fertile,
including rabbits and deer, were released into the Roman Forum
and allowed to run around. The fresco depicts rabbits among
young people, who are kissing and flirting in view of the goddess,
making the tableau suggestive of procreation.

Of roughly the same period are the six wall-length tapestries
known collectively as *The Lady and the Unicorn*, which were
designed in France, woven in Flanders in about 1500, and now
occupy their own room in the Musée de Cluny in Paris. The
first five tapestries are believed to be allegories of the senses:
sight, sound, smell, taste, and touch. The sixth tapestry has been
interpreted as representing the soul or heart. The work is revered
as a French national treasure, and in addition to depicting a lady,
a unicorn, and a lion, the tapestries also feature an abundance
of rabbits. Because the tapestries are enlivened with flowers
and other embellishments, we might be tempted to think that
the small rabbits are merely decorative. But looking closely, it's

possible they might have a more significant role. "The rabbit is the only animal that is present and most frequently depicted in all of the pieces (apart from the lion and the unicorn): it appears 34 times in five different designs (excluding the parts rewoven in the 19th century)," writes Elisabeth Delahaye in her book *The Lady and the Unicorn*. "Yet rabbits were not kept as pets in the Middle Ages. They were wild, and hunted as such." Delahaye, who serves as the general curator of heritage and director of the Musée de Cluny, also notes that the animals were known for their fecundity. "The numerous rabbits scattered over the hanging were perhaps an allusion to carnal love and symbolic of a wish for fertility."

The theme of fertility has a darker turn in a 1726 engraving by editorial cartoonist William Hogarth called *Cunicularii, or the Wise Men of Godliman in Consultation*. Now among the collections of the British Museum in London, a print of the engraving shows an interior scene featuring a woman lying supine on a bed, attended to by a male midwife, and in the process of giving birth to a large number of rabbits. Hogarth's caricature is based on the strange case of Mary Toft, who earlier that year claimed, despite having miscarried a month earlier, that she had gone into labor and produced four rabbits at her home in Godalming, England. Those who believed Mary's astonishing tale—and she did have her supporters, including respected doctors—tried to explain the phenomenon with the theory of maternal impressions, a widely accepted eighteenth-century belief that children would be a physical representation of what their mother was thinking of during conception. It was expected that a "good wife" would be thinking of her husband while procreating, hence the child would share some physical characteristics with the father. The theory also held that emotional stimuli could affect the development of a fetus. Mrs. Toft had allegedly been startled by a rabbit in a field while pregnant, after which she became obsessed with them.

As word spread of Mary's miraculous births, she was brought

to London, where she was interrogated and finally confessed that the whole extraordinary episode was a hoax. Mary spent a few months in prison at Tothill Fields Bridewell, then returned home to Godalming. Somewhat ironically, a decade later she was trudging across a field in Surrey when her foot slipped into a rabbit hole and "she broke her leg in a miserable manner." Mary Toft, "the Rabbit-Woman," died in 1763, her final resting place lost amid the fog of English history.

The bedside drama in *Cunicularii* is both a parody of the Nativity (the first print of the engraving was published at Christmastime) and a satire meant to ridicule the physicians— the "wise men" who were duped by Mary's fraud. ("Godliman" was Hogarth's spelling for her hometown.) The word *cuniculari* is Latin for rabbit-catcher, and here it implies Mary's womb is the equivalent of a rabbit burrow. This would have been well understood in the 1700s, when "coney," a derivative of *cuniculus*, was used to refer to both rabbits and women. So infamous was Mary's case that over the decades a number of other artists, such as John Laguerre and John Faber, portrayed her either holding rabbits or having them escape from beneath her frock. In 1762, Hogarth created another satirical print, *Credulity, Superstition, and Fanaticism*, in which Mary Toft—again shown giving birth to rabbits—is among a dozen references to prevalent delusions.

Earliest Lagomorph Art

Depictions of Paleolithic animals discovered on the limestone walls of caves in France speak to a prehistoric need for humans to comprehend and engage with nature. Within a narrow cave found beneath the village of Gabillou in 1941 is a drawing of a hare that could be 17,000 years old, making it the earliest known piece of lagomorph art. The engraving is in the cave's *Salle du Lièvre*, or "chamber of the hare."

By the 1800s, the European art scene, once closely associated with classical influences, was eagerly embracing nature. Suddenly, rabbits were an ideal subject for art. Typical of these are Johann Georg Seitz's painting *Gemüsestilleben mit Häschen* ("Vegetable Still Life with Rabbits") and *Happy Rabbits* and *Mother Rabbit with Her Babies* by Bernhard te Gempt. Frederick Morgan's painting *Feeding the Rabbits* features a dozen white rabbits in the foreground—and another frolicking in the background. *Rabbits on a Log* by Arthur Fitzwilliam Tait, on exhibit at the Metropolitan Museum of Art in New York City, is especially beautiful in its presentation of three presumably "wild" rabbits (only one of whom is actually on a log) and has been used as the cover of Richard Adams's novel *Tales from Watership Down*, the sequel to his 1972 bestseller. Not to be outdone is John Sherrin, whose exquisite watercolor *Rabbits* depicts a pair of rabbits near their burrow. Like Dürer, Sherrin's brushwork is so richly detailed, with every hair defined, that the painting looks almost like a photograph. No wonder it's hanging in London's Victoria and Albert Museum.

Boy and Rabbit, painted by Scottish artist Henry Raeburn around 1814, is especially significant among many works of this period because the titular bunny is clearly loved as a companion animal and is not presented as symbolic or wild. In this life-sized portrait, a young boy sits beside a white rabbit, who is eating dandelion greens. His right arm is curved protectively around the bunny's body, and he is waiting to feed his friend more of the leaves that he holds in his left hand. We don't know the rabbit's name, but the boy is the artist's step-grandson, Henry Raeburn Inglis, who was about eight years old when he sat for the painting. Young Henry could not hear or speak, and before *Boy and Rabbit* was exhibited at Glasgow's Kelvingrove Art Gallery (on loan from the Royal Academy of Arts) in 2017, curators worked with guides who are Deaf to craft an interpretation panel to accompany the oil painting explaining that "looking after an animal can help people feel calm. There are no communication barriers with animals, and so close friendships can be formed." That certainly seems to be the case in this painting.

British painter Alfred Richardson Barber was uniquely inspired by rabbits and spent much of the late nineteenth century creating such works as *Rabbits, A Frugal Meal, A Mother Rabbit and Her Young, Rabbits Feeding, A Family of Rabbits,* and *The Happy Family,* to name but a few. Sometimes he added another species among the rabbits, such as in *Escaped: Two Rabbits and a Guinea Pig.* Interestingly, all these paintings feature rabbits indoors and eating, and they stress family unity, which begs the question, did Barber have rabbits as companions? It seems very little is known about the artist today beyond the vaguest of biographical details. He was born in 1844 in Colchester, Essex, where he lived most of his life; he raised three children with his wife, Mary; and he died in Suffolk in 1924 at 80 years of age. Apparently unrecorded is what drew Barber to paint rabbits—so many, many rabbits. Did he find their personalities fascinating, for example? Were they artistically challenging? Or was he perhaps merely financially motivated by the eagerness of his Victorian audience to buy live studies featuring these animals? When I contacted the Royal Society of British Artists to enquire about Barber, they admitted they had very little information about him.

An artist we do know much about of course is Beatrix Potter, who filled her books with her own illustrations of rabbits and other animals. A lifelong lover of nature, Beatrix began sketching and painting at an early age, and her subjects were typically the animals in her London home and garden, including not only rabbits but also dogs, caterpillars, frogs, hedgehogs, mice, and birds. Her passion for nature blossomed in her youth, when she and her family (father, mother, younger brother, and her animal friends) would spend summer holidays in Perthshire, Scotland, and in England's idyllic Lake District, where she would eventually relocate. In these locales, time was measured from season to season, rather than moment by moment, and Beatrix was inspired by the unspoiled landscapes and those who occupied them. A natural artist with almost no formal training, she had an eye for precise observation and became an accomplished scientific illustrator, with botanical subjects holding a special fascination for her. Her richly detailed watercolors of mushrooms, most from the 1890s, are so precise that scientists still use them to help identify fungi.

It was in Scotland, staying at Eastwood House on the bucolic River Tay in 1893, that Beatrix wrote and illustrated a letter to her former governess's son Noel Moore, who was recuperating from an illness. In this "picture letter" she told the story of Peter Rabbit, named after her own rabbit, for the first time. The sketches are rudimentary compared to the detailed and colorful renderings of rabbits and other animals she would eventually create for her books, but they must have done wonders to lift the spirits of a five-year-old boy stuck in bed 34 years before the invention of television. Beatrix expanded her letter to Noel a decade later (fortunately he had saved it), and *The Tale of Peter Rabbit* was published in 1902. Eastwood House is not only the birthplace of *Peter Rabbit*; it was also owned by a Scottish laird named Atholl McGregor, whose name may have been the inspiration for the fictional Mr. McGregor.

The year after the publication of *Peter Rabbit*, the Potter family spent their summer holiday in the Lake District, renting a large house on the northwest shore of Derwentwater Lake called Fawe Park, the grounds of which were populated by rabbits, squirrels, birds, frogs, and toads. The animals, along with the estate's greenhouses and elaborate terraced gardens, gave Beatrix the ideal location for *The Tale of Benjamin Bunny*, her 1904 sequel to *Peter Rabbit*. In preparation for the book, she sketched and painted not only the gardens but also the land surrounding the lake. She worked indoors as well, making studies of some of the home's interiors. With Fawe Park's gardens as an artistic guide, the setting of Mr. McGregor's vegetable patch became the Lake District.

Beatrix Potter was influenced by many nineteenth-century illustrators of children's books, among them Randolph Caldecott (1846–86), Walter Crane (1845–1915), and Kate Greenaway (1846–1901). Each was considered a pioneer of the picture book, but Potter scholar Joyce Irene Whalley contends that Caldecott—whose whimsical portraits of animals and household objects inspired the annual Caldecott Medal for distinguished achievement in children's book illustrations—had the most influence on Beatrix's books, in which the pictures enrich or complement the text. "The older artist's work had a simple clarity in the illustrations," she writes, noting that like Beatrix, he used a palette of cool colors and often outlined his drawings in sepia, as did Beatrix in her early work. Caldecott was also important to her because her father collected him, and his works hung in the Potter home.

Whether her subject was flora or fauna, Beatrix excelled at painting or drawing portraits that remain true to the natural world. In her books, she created delightful images (and stories) that reflect her clear understanding of how rabbits behave. So faithful to nature are Peter, his mother, and his sisters that they are familiar to anyone who knows rabbits. Although she anthropomorphized her characters—rendering them with clothes, for instance, and having them speak, shop for baked goods, and drink tea—Beatrix never covered the animals' defining features or changed their anatomy. Absent his shoes and blue jacket, Peter Rabbit would have looked exactly like any other bunny running about the English countryside. As Potter biographer Linda Lear observes: "The illustrations always enhance, rather than distract from or dilute the text, even when a rather sophisticated adult word is introduced. And no matter how beautiful the illustration, the landscape is real, the animals are anatomically accurate, and the plants are planted correctly. It is a triumph of fantasy rooted in fact." (So adamant was Beatrix Potter in her belief that "all writers for children ought to have a sufficient recognition of what things look like" that she criticized *The Wind in the Willows* author Kenneth Grahame for describing the character Mr. Toad as having hair on his head: "A mistake to fly in the face of nature—a frog may wear galoshes; but I don't hold with toads having beards or wigs!")

Beatrix included rabbits in other works, too, such as her 1909 book *The Tale of Ginger and Pickles*, in which a cat (Ginger) and a dog (Pickles) are partners in a popular village shop that carries groceries and other provisions. It is clear that all of her stories are set in the same world, so it is no surprise to find that the shop's customers include Peter Rabbit and his cousin Benjamin Bunny, as well as many mice from other Potter tales. The rabbits are depicted looking very wary around Pickles, and Ginger refuses to help the mice, fearing he will be tempted to eat them. Under the circumstances, such proprietors were probably doomed to fail, but fortunately for the villagers, the shop is eventually operated by a hen, and the customers are immediately put at ease. Like much of what Beatrix painted, the business is based on an actual shop in her local Lake District village, and the residents were delighted to see scenes from their community portrayed in the book.

In Peter's Image

In 1979, to commemorate the International Year of the Child, the UK's Royal Mail issued a nine-pence Peter Rabbit postage stamp. Other countries have since created stamps with Peter's likeness, including Japan, the Solomon Islands, and Liberia. Apparently, Liberia didn't think the original Peter looked elegant enough and designed their own version, with a rabbit sporting a walking stick, long coat, and pince-nez spectacles. In 2016, to mark 150 years since Beatrix Potter's birth, Peter hopped into British currency on a limited-edition 50-pence piece, the first time a character from children's literature has appeared on UK coinage. Not to be outdone, the Royal Mail released four new Peter Rabbit stamps that same year, also in celebration of the author.

When she died in 1943 at the age of 77, Beatrix Potter bequeathed more than 4000 acres (1600 hectares) in the Lake District, including the home she bought in 1905, to Britain's National Trust, ensuring the landscape that inspired her work would be preserved. And she left us all a legacy of 23 books that have never gone out of print—and an enduring symbol of rabbitude.

Asian artists have a long tradition of making animals the center of their work, and lagomorphs are a popular theme. Carving jade is an especially popular medium in Chinese culture, where for more than 7000 years this green mineral has been used to create symbolic and ritual objects in many forms, including rabbits and hares. On display in the Asian Art Museum in San Francisco is one example: a small pendant in the shape of a hare that was carved during the Western Zhou period (about 1050–771 BCE).

Prolific Chinese master Qi Baishi drew inspiration from nature, and his graceful ink-brush paintings of rabbits and other animals reflect his distinctive *da xieyi* style, a technique that places emphasis on expressing the spirit of the subject rather than accuracy or detail. Several of his most famous rabbit paintings are remarkably similar. *Sweet Osmanthus and Rabbits* (1938), *Rabbits and Osmanthus* (1943), *Rabbits Under Osmanthus Tree* (1946), *Two Rabbits* (1948), and *Rabbit and Laurel Blossom* (undated) all feature one black and one pink-eyed white rabbit—presumably mates—huddled together beneath tree branches. There are no backgrounds or indeed any surface for the rabbits to sit upon; the focus is purely on the flora and fauna. Each is painted on a long scroll and evokes a feeling of calmness. They are also considered investments: in 2014, *Rabbits Under Osmanthus Tree* sold at auction for US$383,500.

In late-eighteenth-century Japan, Maruyama Okyo created colorful, mesmerizing woodblock prints of rabbits. Founder of the Maruyama school of painting, Okyo focused on naturalism—according to legend, he once painted the portrait of a ghost so realistically that it suddenly materialized and terrified him. Much less frightening are his paintings of rabbits, who occupy serene spaces in nature settings. *Mokuzoku and Rabbits*, one of his most famous works, is a tranquil portrait of three rabbits on a small hill, relaxed yet alert. *Rabbits Seated Together*, with one black and one white rabbit, could have easily inspired the work of Qi Baishi.

Rabbits also appear in the famous *Choju-giga*, or "animal caricatures," belonging to Kyoto's Kozan-ji temple. Painted onto four scrolls, the images of anthropomorphic rabbits frolicking with frogs and monkeys are thought to have been created in the twelfth and thirteenth centuries, making them perhaps the first examples of manga, or Japanese comics. In 2009, the Kyoto National Museum began to restore the scrolls and completed the work in 2014.

The tradition of creating works of art that showcase rabbits (and hares, of course) continues unabated throughout the world. Among my favorites are the works of wildlife artist Marion Rose, who worked in acrylic and oil and used bold brushstrokes and unexpected colors to paint dramatic portraits of rabbits and hares. Her work *Forest Bunny*, for instance, features an alert rabbit rendered in hues of pink, blue, green, purple, yellow, orange, and red. Seated in vegetation, the bunny is surrounded by the golden colors of autumn. Marion passed away in 2011, but her husband Garry told me that she spent most of her life in the country and observed rabbits and other animals from their motorhome, which wildlife seemed drawn to.

Sam Cannon is an artist living in Dorset, England, and works in watercolors, gouache, color pencils, and graphite pencil. Her stylized depictions of animals such as hares frequently feature a bit of text—often a quotation or part of a poem. "I'll choose a subject and then there will be all my lists of poems and quotes surrounding me," she explains. "Well, the ones I want to use the most. And hopefully I'll be able to marry the two together." The results are quite moving. In one of her paintings, two hares rest among a field of daisies and are accompanied by the words of poet John Keats: "My love is selfish. I cannot breathe without you." In another, an adult hare and juvenile sit beneath the glow of the moon. Below them is a line from novelist Honoré de Balzac: "The heart of a mother is a deep abyss at the bottom of which you will always find forgiveness." Often the hares sit with their foreheads pressed together; sometimes the subject is a lone hare. "I love the shapes they make," Sam says. "I love their long ears and the fact that you can capture them running, lounging, sitting up staring, boxing, grooming themselves. All fantastic shapes to capture."

Perhaps the modern artist most celebrated for their rabbit-related works is Hunt Slonem, who began painting rabbits in the 1970s. Reflecting the innocence of his subject, his works are playful and almost childlike, rendered with sweeping brushstrokes on solid-color backgrounds such as red, yellow, blue, pink, green, and white. The artist has felt a connection with rabbits since his childhood, when his parents put two of them in a backyard hutch. "Their names were Pixie and Barnaby, and they got me into all kinds of trouble," he says. That's because young Hunt brought his furry friends into the house to play. "They were *not* litter box trained, so they'd soil the sofa," he explains with a chuckle.

When he moved to New York in the '70s, the deeply spiritual artist began painting Catholic saints, and he'd feature animals at their feet, including rabbits. These early works are much more detailed than the rabbit images he creates now, which are roughly delineated outlines meant to suggest rather than overtly state rabbitness. His 1983 portrait of Saint Martin de Porres, for instance, features five beautifully rendered Dutch bunnies in the lower corner. Hunt says he began painting rabbits by themselves in the late 1980s or early '90s. It was around this time that he discovered something perhaps not surprising. "I was at a restaurant late one night in Chinatown in New York, and learned a bit about the Chinese zodiac," he says. "I realized I am the sign of the Rabbit."

Hunt begins every morning at his waterfront Brooklyn studio by taking a stack of rectangular pieces of wood or Masonite, each one 8 by 10 inches (20 x 25 cm), and painting bunnies on them. This is how he warms up for a day of creating. "I paint four, five, or six every morning," he says. Each of these he sets in one of the many antique frames that he's amassed from flea markets over the years and then hangs them in his home studio, salon style. "They sell all the time," he says. Asked why rabbits have inspired him so much, he pauses for a moment. "I always thought they were wonderful animals," he says.

On larger canvases, Hunt's paintings often feature the kind of repeated images—row after row of, say, rabbits or tropical birds—that is indicative of pop art, though he's actually part of the neo-expressionist movement, which emerged in the late 1970s as a rough painting style that embraces bold colors. He says that his Warhol-like repetition of a particular subject isn't so much pop art as a way to remind the viewer to take a last look at nature, which is rapidly disappearing.

Hunt's paintings fetch many thousands of dollars each, and they can be found in the permanent collections of museums around the world. His bunnies also adorn wallpaper, furniture upholstery, and even men's swimming trunks. And they appear in some of his public works of art, including a colorful sculpture called *Bunny Hop*. The tower of rabbit silhouettes, cut from aluminum and painted in primary and secondary colors, is among the works beautifying a green space in Kenner, Louisiana.

Newcastle's Vampire Rabbit

Crouching high above an ornate arched doorway of the Cathedral Buildings adjacent to St. Nicholas's Churchyard in Newcastle-upon-Tyne, England, is a mysterious rabbit sculpture. With bared fangs, sharp claws, and fearsome eyes, the carving has become known as the Vampire Rabbit. Created in 1901 when the buildings were erected, the rabbit used to have shorter ears and was the same sandy color as the surrounding stonework; he's since been painted black and the ears are much longer (someone supposedly replaced the original set that a builder had knocked off). No one is sure why the sculpture, officially called a grotesque, was put there, but one legend says that because the Vampire Rabbit overlooks what was once the cathedral's cemetery (now a car park), his spooky presence was meant to ward off grave robbers.

While public art featuring lagomorphs is not particularly common—the large hare sculpture by Ottmar Hörl beside the Vienna State Opera being another bright and notable exception— an art project in Berlin shines a poignant light on a dark period of European history. In 1961, the Communist government of East Germany began constructing a barrier between East and West Berlin that served to reduce the defections from East to West that had been occurring since the city was divided in 1945 following World War II. The Berlin Wall cut residents off from family, friends, jobs, schools, and many other aspects of their daily lives. It completely surrounded West Berlin and was eventually constructed as two parallel walls. The walls were 90 miles (145 km) long with a broad space in between, ranging from 30 to 100 yards (27–90 m) wide, that was referred to as "no-man's-land." It was also called the "death strip," since refugees who crossed, or attempted to cross, the fortified border risked being shot by guards or killed by mines. Estimates vary on how many escapees died during the 28 years the barricade stood, but the Berlin Wall Memorial lists 140.

Another population that was affected were the thousands of wild rabbits who had helped themselves to the communal vegetable gardens of the devastated post-war city and flourished as urban dwellers. When the Wall went up, the rabbit colonies were cut off too. But they did what bunnies do and tunneled beneath the political boundary, indulging an instinctual freedom that their human neighbors were denied. Many rabbits found themselves in the wilderness of no-man's-land—to them a grass-covered sanctuary free of hunters and ground predators—and chose to stay. The rabbits enjoyed a generally peaceful life, according to reports (they were too light to set off the mines), yet they faced an uncertain future when the Wall came down in 1989 and their beloved green belt was soon overrun with people. Most of the leporine Berliners migrated west, navigating a metropolis they were wholly unprepared for.

In 1996, the city invited 35 local artists to propose ideas for public art installations that would commemorate the Berlin Wall in some way. Among the eight artists chosen was Karla Sachse, who had grown up during the Cold War and once lived in an apartment overlooking the Wall's eastern side, where she could see the rabbits from her window. "I always knew—a bit jealously—that rabbits could dig tunnels to live in the West or East or between the two walls of the Wall," she says. Perhaps not surprisingly, Karla chose rabbits as the subject for her art project: 120 life-sized silhouettes of hopping, crouching, and sitting bunnies forged in brass. Calling her work *Kaninchenfeld* ("Rabbit Field"), she installed the silhouettes in and around the street and sidewalks at the intersection of Chausseestrasse and Liesenstrasse, which had served as a border-crossing site for residents who had an approved reason to come and go. Karla explains that she picked the location because it was here that she would greet the eight-year-old friend of her son. "Her parents had moved from East Berlin to West Berlin and were not allowed to return to the East," she says. "Only their little daughter could cross the border to visit her grandmother and my son. The poor child had to pass the armed guards on this long-distance checkpoint totally alone, over and back, with her mother and me on both ends waving at each other."

In selecting Karla's project, the competition's jury acknowledged that initially her submission didn't seem to embrace the significance of the competition theme. Yet ultimately, they agreed, she had proposed an inspired work, writing: "The reference to rabbits, the noble hare's smaller cousins, as the peaceful and subversive inhabitants of this deadly strip of land hints at an approach that is taken up again in the ornamental treatment of the street space." *Kaninchenfeld* was completed in 1999, in time for the ten-year anniversary of the unification of Germany, but road work and building construction has since resulted in the loss of many of the rabbit silhouettes. "There are only about sixty figures left," says Karla. "But the cultural authorities of the town are willing to replace at least forty rabbits so that there are plenty again." She adds that the former checkpoint may soon be better marked, as well, "with two explanatory pillars on each end of the 'rabbit field.'"

Karla Sachse's work isn't the only form of art dedicated to the rabbits of the Berlin Wall. In 2009, Polish filmmaker Bartosz Konopka released his documentary short *Rabbit à la Berlin*, which views the East–West tension through the eyes of the rabbits who occupied no-man's-land and was nominated for an Academy Award. The story also makes an appearance in a 1993 German children's book by Irene Dische and Hans Magnus Enzensberger called *Esterhazy*, about a rabbit who goes to Berlin in search of a mate and witnesses the destruction of the Berlin Wall. Among the many beautiful paintings by Michael Sowa in the 2009 English edition is a colorful image of a dozen or so carefree rabbits dressed in human clothes lounging in the shadow of the Wall.

Arguably the most unusual piece of lagomorph-inspired art, modern or otherwise, comes from Dieter Roth, a Swiss artist whose 1968 work *Karnickelköttelkarnickel* ("Bunny-Dropping Bunny") imitates the shape of a chocolate Easter Bunny. Rather than being made of a delicious confection, however, Roth's sculpture is composed of rabbit excrement and held together with bits of straw. A mere 7 inches tall (18 cm), *Bunny* is meant to exhibit the organic process of decay. Roth created hundreds more copies of the piece for sale over the next seven years, many of which leave the fecal pellets discernibly round and thus more obvious what the work was composed of.

It is little wonder that rabbits have influenced artists for thousands of years, when humans first captured the essence of these animals with primitive paintings on the walls of caves. Ask any artist, and they will tell you how they are inspired by their shape, their gracefulness, and their furtive nature. Today there is no visual art form, from intricate watercolor portraits to abstract sculptures, that has not in some way embodied the rabbit. Even creators of film and television, undoubtedly the art form with the largest mass appeal, are captivated by rabbits, telling their stories on modern canvases around the world. As we will see, it's just one element of making the rabbit a pop-culture icon.

Chapter Six

Rabbits in Popular Culture

"Hallo, Rabbit," he said, "is that you?"
"Let's pretend it isn't," said Rabbit, "and see what happens."
—A. A. Milne, *Winnie-the-Pooh*

As Peter Rabbit and the Easter Bunny so ably demonstrate, rabbits have a special place in literature, movies, television, and even marketing (the advertising agency behind the Energizer Bunny, for instance, chose a rabbit because of the animal's clear association with endurance, renewal, playfulness, and potency). The cultural influence of mass media means that most of us are aware of Bugs Bunny and the White Rabbit from *Alice in Wonderland*. Likewise, you've probably seen Disney's *Bambi* and might have been as impressed as I was by Thumper's ice-skating skills, or perhaps you sobbed over Richard Adams's 1972 novel *Watership Down*. You may count Rabbit from the *Winnie-the-Pooh* stories by A. A. Milne as your favorite lagomorph character or maybe even Roger Rabbit (though doubtfully). And we can only wonder how many children have heaped affection on their rabbit stuffies in the hope of bringing them to life, as in the immensely popular 1922 book *The Velveteen Rabbit* by Margery Williams.

To really understand the significance of rabbits in popular media today, it's important to go back to the beginning of the motion picture industry, when rabbits originally became an important motif for filmmakers. Among the earliest examples is a 1903 film produced in England called *Alice in Wonderland*. The first screen adaptation of Lewis Carroll's book *Alice's Adventures in Wonderland*, the 12-minute silent feature depicts key moments from the story, such as Alice chasing the waistcoat-wearing White Rabbit (a costumed actor) down a rabbit hole and later enjoying a tea party with other guests, including the March Hare, who appears much as he does in John Tenniel's original illustrations for the novel. The only known copy of this visually innovative short film, which was the longest yet produced in Britain, had deteriorated considerably over the decades and was restored by the British Film Institute in 2010, although four minutes of the original have been lost.

By the 1920s, standard movies were getting longer, though the running time of animated films—still an emerging technology—remained only a few minutes. These cartoon shorts relied on the same broad acting and sight gags as their live-action counterparts, but animators could realize virtually any scene or action and make animals the principal characters. Thus it was in the 1920s that Walt Disney found his first successes creating animated films that were shown before the main feature in cinemas. Mickey Mouse would make his theatrical debut in 1928, but a year prior, Disney's star was Oswald the Lucky Rabbit. At this time, animated felines were all the rage (particularly Felix the Cat and Krazy Kat), and Disney wanted his rabbit character to be imbued with more personality, to have a unique style beyond a superficial habit or mannerism. Over the span of 26 short films, Oswald's ingenuity, pluck, and cheerfulness would help him transcend the personas of many of his contemporaries—and become the template for Mickey. Although the character's physical appearance changed slightly over the series, Oswald was generally dressed simply in short pants, sometimes held up by a lone suspender.

Inspired by the onscreen exploits of actors Harold Lloyd and Buster Keaton, Oswald was placed in situations where his resourcefulness would save him. Sadly, many of these early silent cartoons have been lost, but a typical example is the 1927 short *Trolley Troubles*, in which Oswald is the operator of a streetcar loaded with bunny passengers that strains to make it up a steep incline. Spotting a goat on the track, Oswald tricks the animal into head-butting the car up and over the hill. The trolley then careens, roller coaster-style, through a series of curves, ejecting all the passengers along the way. Frantic, Oswald pops off his own foot, kisses it, rubs it on his head, then reattaches it—playing on the trope that a rabbit's foot is lucky. (The character's ability to remove, stretch, and morph his body parts would become a running gag.) Oswald finally ends up in a river using the streetcar as a raft.

Oswald the Lucky Rabbit was a huge hit, and his name began appearing on theater marquees and newspaper ads alongside feature films. He was also Disney's first marketing success, with his likeness being sold on buttons, stickers, stencil sets, a wind-up doll, and other merchandise. The Oswald cartoons are rudimentary by today's standards, but they are unquestionably inventive and brimming with enthusiasm. It's easy to see why audiences in the 1920s became so fond of this rabbit and why, a century later, he retains pride of place in the lineup of Disney stars. (Walt Disney lost the rights to Oswald in 1928, but his company regained them in 2006, 40 years after his death.)

It's safe to say that if it weren't for Oswald, there would have been no Crusader Rabbit. What—you've never heard of Crusader Rabbit? Oh, please sit back while I tell you about this groundbreaking bunny.

Setting the stage for shows like *The Flintstones* and *The Simpsons, Crusader Rabbit* was the first animated series created specifically for television, test marketed in 1948. Television was still a novel medium then—regular TV broadcasts had only begun four years earlier with NBC; ABC and CBS followed in 1948. The audience was small: in the United States, there were fewer than 50,000 television sets, each producing a blue-and-gray glow that would represent the state of the art in mid-century technology. There wasn't much on, but of what was available to watch, children's shows like *Howdy Doody* and *Kukla, Fran and Ollie* were popular, and very short cartoons could be used as filler (think *The Itchy and Scratchy Show* on *The Krusty the Clown Show* on *The Simpsons*).

To save money and time, *Crusader Rabbit* co-producers Alex Anderson and Jay Ward used "limited" animation, a technique they would also employ in their next show, *The Adventures of Rocky and Bullwinkle and Friends*. The movement in the cartoons is crude and more like narrated storyboards than a true animated series. But even with choppy motion, filmed in black and white, it's clear that Crusader is brave and clever. In his first 15-episodes adventure, "Crusader vs. the State of Texas," he liberates a tiger named Rags from a circus cage by picking the lock, and the two head to Texas to stop the harassment and deportation of rabbits and hares, who are eating every carrot in the state.

Like *Rocky and Bullwinkle*, much of the humor here is aimed at adults as well as children. In one episode, for example, a school of fishes use their protruding upper jawbones in the shape of can openers to sink an ironclad ship called the *Robert E. Leak*. The original *Crusader Rabbit* lasted 195 episodes, ending production in 1951, but the rabbit was revived in 1957 to fight injustice for another 260 episodes in color, even though black-and-white TVs would remain the standard until the mid 1960s.

Hoppy Rabbit Day
Every year on the fourth Saturday of September, International Rabbit Day promotes the protection and care of wild and domesticated rabbits.

A world apart from both *Oswald* and *Crusader Rabbit*, both in scope and artistic achievement, is *The Curse of the Were-Rabbit*, a 2005 stop-motion animated mystery–horror–comedy feature film produced by the filmmakers behind *Chicken Run* (2000). Part *Wolf Man* and part *Dr. Jekyll and Mr. Hyde*, Were-Rabbit centers on inventor Wallace and his canine friend Gromit, who are summoned to Tottington Hall to humanely catch a colony of rabbits who have been devouring Lady Tottington's vegetable garden just days before the town's annual Giant Vegetable Competition.

The trouble begins when Wallace tries to rid the rabbits of their "antisocial veg-ravaging behavior" by subjecting them to his latest invention: a brainwashing machine called the Mind Manipulation-O-Matic, which he operates beneath the glow of a full moon. It's all done in the spirit of compassion, but when one of the buns goes cranium-to-cranium with Wallace as the device is on full power, he absorbs the inventor's distaste for vegetables, while Wallace gradually adopts lagomorph characteristics. Soon the town has a much larger problem to cope with, as a giant rabbit goes on a rampage through everyone's obsessively tended veggie gardens. What makes the story shine are characters so fully realized that you forget you're watching a film that required five years of work with animators carefully manipulating the movement of clay models frame by frame. And as the perfect finale, Tottington Hall and its expansive grounds are transformed into a sanctuary for rabbits. *The Curse of the Were-Rabbit* won an Academy Award for Best Animated Feature, and *The Guinness Book of World Records* says it required more Plasticine (a brand of modeling clay) than any other film in history: 6272 pounds (2845 kg).

No animated rabbit, however, matches the popularity of Bugs Bunny. In fact, even though most of the shorts he starred in were produced before 1960 (his official first appearance was a 1940 short called *A Wild Hare*), Bugs is consistently ranked as the most famous rabbit in popular culture and the most popular cartoon character in the USA, largely due to his appearances on television beginning in the 1960s. According to *The Guinness Book of World Records*, he has appeared in more films (both short and full-length) than any other cartoon character. The bulk of these films came out of the Warner Bros. studio in Hollywood, where Bugs Bunny was voiced by Mel Blanc. "He's a little stinker," Blanc once said of Bugs. "He does what most people would like to do but don't have the guts to do."

Unfortunately, he might seem like a mere "stinker," but Bugs is deeply rooted in racism, and as we explore the role of rabbits in pop culture, it's important we don't ignore a troubling history of this character that is rarely discussed. Said to be inspired by Groucho Marx as well as Clark Gable's carrot-chomping scene in *It Happened One Night* (1934), Bugs Bunny was much more influenced by the practice of blackface minstrelsy—traditionally a white performer perpetuating a host of racist stereotypes (an unruly trickster resistant to work and social norms, for example) that long affected how white people viewed Black people. According to media scholar Nicholas Sammond, author of *Birth of an Industry: Blackface Minstrelsy and the Rise of American Animation*, minstrelsy was an immensely popular form of entertainment, and early animators borrowed liberally from it. Just two examples of this are a 1941 propaganda short called *Any Bonds Today*, which features Bugs in blackface singing "Sammy" (as in Uncle Sam), a pastiche of the Al Jolson song "Mammy," and *Southern Fried Rabbit* (1953), with Bugs posing as an enslaved person. Some other Bugs Bunny cartoons, such as *All This and Rabbit Stew* (1941), depict Blacks as dimwitted, with grossly exaggerated lips and lazy mannerisms.

"Bugs Bunny is definitely part of the tradition of stories in which small characters defeat larger ones through intellect, and the stories that enslaved adults told their children often cast rabbits as the smaller, heroic characters," says ethnic studies professor Christopher Lehman, author of *The Colored Cartoon:*

Black Representation in American Animated Short Films, 1907–1954. "It's important to acknowledge that the use of Bugs by Warner Bros. to outwit African-American stereotypes in *All This and Rabbit Stew* and Bugs's use of blackface in *Any Bonds Today* and *Southern Fried Rabbit* complicate the tradition in a very ironic way."

Dr. Lehman also notes that Bugs Bunny's lineage can be traced to Br'er Rabbit, the trickster character author Joel Chandler Harris appropriated from stories told by enslaved African-Americans for his book *Uncle Remus: His Songs and His Sayings*, published in 1880. "Indeed," writes Dr. Lehman, "both characters share the traits of confidence and cleverness, and both are willing to feign humility in the process of outsmarting their adversaries." He observes that Bugs Bunny's folktale roots are also illustrated by his generosity, as when he allows Elmer Fudd in *A Wild Hare* to believe he has been successful in his hunt. "Br'er Rabbit does the same thing in *Uncle Remus*, convincingly pleading with his captor not to throw him into the briar patch he calls 'home.'" Dr. Lehman points out that even Bugs Bunny's famous line "What's up, Doc?" is a direct descendant of the coded language Black men and women used when confronted with racism—a way of disarming the situation without being confrontational.

Some Bugs Bunny shorts have since had offensive scenes edited out—or been dropped from syndication altogether—although that doesn't help address the character's racist roots. Again, as we acknowledge the influence of real rabbits on popular culture, we must not ignore or excuse characterizations that can be hurtful.

And what more can be said about Br'er Rabbit, one of the central characters in *Uncle Remus*? As a figure of nineteenth-century children's literature, Br'er Rabbit has certainly found a place in the history of popular culture. He's an archetypal trickster who consistently outwits his foes. Yet it's difficult to get past the book's introduction, in which Harris asks readers to believe that the Uncle Remus character, the narrative's storyteller who was once enslaved, "has nothing but pleasant memories of the discipline of slavery."

But most people today probably know Br'er Rabbit from the animated/live-action adaptation of these stories, Walt Disney's 1946 feature *Song of the South*, or the children's books the movie was adapted into. The film is set in post–Civil War Georgia and depicts Uncle Remus living a highly romanticized version of plantation life. In one of the scenes taken directly from the book, Br'er Fox tricks Br'er Rabbit into becoming entangled with a doll covered in tar. This leads to Br'er Rabbit appearing as if he's in blackface. Last seen theatrically in 1986, *Song of the South* with its animated Br'er Rabbit (br'er is an abbreviation of brother) has never been available in the USA on any home video format. Like certain Bugs Bunny cartoons, Disney executives decided that the film was "fairly offensive" and would keep it locked away.

Not all pop-culture rabbits are animated of course—or even visible. Watching the comedy film *Harvey*, you have to use your imagination to see the title character, although he's described as standing more than 6 feet (1.8 m) tall. Harvey is a white rabbit and friend of Elwood P. Dowd, played by James Stewart. Gentle and well-mannered, Elwood is portrayed as an eccentric nonconformist not quite at home in a society with a proclivity for suppressing individuality. Because no one else but Elwood can see Harvey, we're led to believe that he only thinks he sees him. But as the story progresses, the truth of Harvey becomes evident.

Elwood spends most days down at the local pub with his imperceptible lapin pal, drinking martinis and making friends. It is here that Elwood seems most at home, perhaps because the bartender and regular patrons fully accept Harvey and appreciate Elwood. Elwood's sister, on the other hand, considers her brother an embarrassment, and the narrative takes a dramatic turn when she tries to have him committed to a sanitarium. As the churlish medical staff spend time with Elwood, however, they come to believe in Harvey, too, and grow into nicer people.

Harvey began life as a play written by Mary Chase, and it won a Pulitzer Prize for drama in 1945. Chase was born to Irish parents and describes Harvey as a pooka—a Celtic spirit in animal form who can only be seen by those who believe in them. In addition to invisibility, Harvey has the power to stop clocks and then, as Elwood explains, "you can go anywhere you like, with anyone you like, and stay as long as you like, and when you get back, not one minute will have ticked by." (Again the association of rabbits with magic.) By the end of the story, Harvey has become real to everyone. Not surprisingly, Stewart thought of *Harvey* as one of the best films he made.

Because rabbits are so often equated with childhood and innocence, media creators sometimes twist that perception for humorous effect, giving the public lagomorphic characters whose actions or mere presence belie their symbolic benevolence. Pushing this trope even further is the 1975 film *Monty Python and the Holy Grail* and its Killer Rabbit of Caerbannog—"the most foul, cruel, and bad-tempered rodent you ever set eyes on!" In a key scene, King Arthur and his knights ignore the warnings about this "monster" rabbit, who emerges from a cave and quickly begins attacking them, forcing the king to shout "Run away!" The inspiration for this cinematic moment seems to be the Allegory of Cowardice sculpture found at Notre Dame cathedral in Paris. Carved in about 1230, this relief panel depicts a knight who has dropped his sword and is retreating from an aggressive rabbit. Images like this were a popular theme in medieval Europe, where teachings against the vice of cowardice often featured heavily armed knights fleeing from harmless animals like snails and rabbits.

Coney Cocktail

Rabbits have such a notable presence in popular culture that it's no surprise to find drinks named after them. One such libation is the veggie-infused Killer Rabbit of Caerbannog cocktail.

Ingredients:

½ ounce Pimm's
½ ounce Scotch
1 ounce carrot juice
½ ounce cucumber juice, extracted
½ ounce lemon juice
½ ounce simple syrup (1:1, sugar:water)
soda, to top

Directions:
Combine all ingredients in shaker and shake. Pour over ice into a beer mug, top with soda, and garnish with strawberry, cucumber, and mint. Serves one.

Monks in the Middle Ages apparently got the joke as well, and they entertained themselves by illustrating small, colorful, subversive doodles in decorative margins called drolleries. Painted in illuminated manuscripts (so called because of the gold and silver used), drolleries typically favored animal–human hybrids and mythical creatures like dragons and griffins. But some monks used these handwritten books to illustrate rabbits and hares wielding axes and swords, severing heads, killing knights, and engaging in other forms of mayhem. Christopher de Hamel, perhaps the world's leading expert on illuminated manuscripts, says these farcical drawings of otherwise amiable animals represent "the reversal of normality, the world turned upside down—that silent and meek hares mercilessly hunted by humans should become armed with bows and arrows and turn violently on us." Depictions of lagomorphs exacting their revenge evidently amused the artists, and this motif was not limited to medieval marginalia. Indeed, among the fifteenth-century wooden carvings that support the choir stalls in England's Manchester Cathedral is one in which rabbits are roasting a hunter on a spit while cooking his dogs in a pot; we can only guess how that found a home beneath the bums of the choir and clergy.

Such imagery has not only survived the centuries but also influences nonconformist media today, with many rabbit-themed amusements marketed for mature consumers. In *Donnie Darko*, a science fiction–mystery film released in 2001, a teenaged boy is haunted by visions of a man in a disturbing rabbit costume, who urges him to commit destructive acts. In addition to the guy in the creepy bunny suit, other "rabbits" featured in the movie include a Volkswagen Rabbit, a plush rabbit toy, a frightening jack-o'-lantern shaped like a rabbit's head, and music by the English band Echo & the Bunnymen.

It is arguably the sort of sinister weirdness permeating *Donnie Darko* that the producers of *Night of the Lepus* were hoping to achieve with their 1972 film about giant rabbits terrorizing an Arizona town. When an effort to use an untested serum to control the population of wild rabbits on a local ranch goes horribly, predictably wrong, it's up to the stalwart townsfolk to deal with a horde of rabbits who have each grown to the size of a fully loaded SUV. Trouble is, the special effects are anything but special, so there is no sense the rabbits have become the huge, bloodthirsty beasts they are supposed to be. They are not even wild rabbits but domesticated bunnies who are placed on miniature sets and appear more sleepy than sinister. Sometimes what we see is just an actor in a bunny costume displaying all the menace of a shag carpet. Though it strives to be a horror film about ecological balance and the consequences of genetic manipulation, *Night of the Lepus* comes off as pure farce.

Made in an era when mutant critters running amuck sold movie tickets (think *Willard*, *Frogs*, or *Empire of the Ants*), *Night of the Lepus* is loosely based on the satirical science fiction novel *The Year of the Angry Rabbit* by Russell Braddon. But while the book is played for laughs, the filmmakers removed all the humor and tried to turn bunnies into villains, resulting in a shlocky B-movie whose cast earnestly struggles to overcome the ludicrous premise and technical laziness that invites viewers to imagine a colony of cuddly conies doing any damage beyond biting through the occasional telephone line. When a peace officer pulls into a drive-in theater and announces to the patrons, "Ladies and gentlemen, attention! There is a herd of killer rabbits headed this way," it's easy to hear the audience still snickering decades later.

The idea of rampaging rabbits looked good on paper, *Lepus* star Janet Leigh revealed years later, though she and her co-stars realized a few days into shooting that the movie was hopeless. "You just want to burst out laughing because you have this herd of giant rabbits that are supposed to be menacing, and they're *bunny rabbits*. There was nothing we could do to make them frightening," she said, admitting in another interview, "I've forgotten as much as I could about that picture." Tellingly, the studio behind the movie, MGM, seemed to recognize the preposterous flop they had on their hands, and they left out any reference to rabbits in their marketing—well, other than the word Lepus, a clue likely lost on most moviegoers. Instead, one poster shows a woman cowering beneath the shadow of a monster with sharp fangs while another depicts a set of large eyes accompanied by the text "Killing, eating as they prowl … Growing larger as they eat. A nightmare born that tragic moment when Science made its great mistake." Not even the movie's trailer shows a rabbit clearly.

Much more successful in the creepiness camp is *Inland Empire*, a 2006 film by David Lynch. Because most of Lynch's projects are distinctly surreal and without the kind of conventional narrative devices movie and TV audiences have come to expect—such as a coherent plot—it's often difficult to pinpoint exactly what the director is trying to say or even allude to. That can make his films seem all the more unsettling, which is undoubtedly his intention. And so within *Inland Empire* he presents scenes of three rabbits who are so anthropomorphized that they appear to be more human than leporine. There is a female rabbit who is ironing when we first see her, another female rabbit who is sitting on a couch, and a male rabbit who, upon entering the scene, is greeted with canned applause. All the action and dialog, what little there is of either, takes place in the front room of a house or apartment. When the rabbits speak, they converse in non sequiturs, which sound eerie yet are often followed by a laugh track. All of this is seen through the eyes of a distressed female character, who is watching the rabbits on television. What it has to do with the overall arc of *Inland Empire* is really a matter of opinion, although the rabbit sitcom reflects some elements that came before it in the movie and could be a commentary on banal TV shows.

Lynch—for whom avant-garde is more like a cloak than a label—incorporated the *Inland Empire* rabbit scenes from his 2002 web series *Rabbits,* in which three actors wearing brown rabbit heads speak of secrets and dread. Not exactly the world of Peter Rabbit here. They could represent two women and a man who can nearly manifest in rabbit form, or they might be three rabbits who can almost pull off a human look (the male rabbit wears a business suit, for instance). Whatever the case, there is something distinctly haunting and unnerving about the rabbits in these scenes, and it makes for some truly disturbing viewing.

Among the many filmmakers who acknowledge David Lynch as an artistic influence is Jordan Peele, who got audiences talking about rabbits with the release of his horror film *Us* in 2019. Rabbits are featured prominently throughout the movie; even as the opening credits play out, the camera focuses on one bunny in a cage and slowly pulls back to reveal dozens more (a character refers to these rabbits as a food source). There is a plush toy rabbit at the cabin where much of the story develops, and one of the main characters wears a T-shirt with a bunny design and later a sweatshirt bearing the word *Thỏ*, which is Vietnamese for rabbit. The rabbit motif is presented more playfully when another important character follows a white rabbit into a series of staircases, leading her down a proverbial rabbit hole. Indeed, the film's labyrinth of tunnels neatly mirrors the burrows rabbits build in the wild. We can even see a similarity between the long ears of the many rabbits and the many pairs of dressmaker's scissors that are central to the narrative. Finally, in the last scene, a third character gently cradles a bunny rescued from the subterranean world.

It's natural to wonder why Peele, a director known for his meticulous use of symbolism in his storytelling, would choose rabbits as such a prominent trope. He said he approached *Us* as a "dark Easter" tale focusing on a messiah figure who, having been left for dead, returns. Rabbits represent rebirth, which is another important theme of *Us*, and in this film they also parallel in some ways the fate of key characters, who go from being victims without agency to being liberated and able to move about where they please.

Beneath the surface of *Us*, both figuratively and literally, are the remnants of a failed scientific experiment that has been abandoned, the discovery of which is foreshadowed when the character who favors rabbit-themed fashions tells her family that the US government puts fluoride in the water supply to control the populace. Such references to government experiments take on another layer of meaning when you remember how some rabbits have been used historically. In this way, a further interpretation is that the underworld of *Us* parallels Okunoshima, a small island the Japanese government used for developing poison gases in the 1930s and '40s and then deserted; now nicknamed *Usagi Jima* ("Rabbit Island"), it is home to hundreds of feral rabbits, supposedly the descendants of eight domesticated bunnies released on the island by schoolchildren in the 1970s.

Funny Bunny

Like many other pop-culture icons, rabbits have been featured in many jokes, riddles, and puns. Here's one I particularly like:

A priest, a minister, and a rabbit walk into a bar. The rabbit says, "I think I might be a typo."

On the other end of the tone spectrum is the animated series *30 Second Bunnies Theatre*, in which anthropomorphic, fast-talking rabbits act out key scenes from movies such as *Die Hard*, *The Birds*, *Jaws*, *Star Wars*, and *The Exorcist*. Although everything is played for laughs, the scenes are sometimes violent, but because the rabbits are acting like their human counterparts, it seems much more palatable. An Internet sensation when it premiered in 2004, the series is still popular, with a growing list of shorts online, each with a title card declaring "A movie parody in Bun-O-Vision!"

Rabbits have been a major presence in comic books as well, where they have been cast as superheroes. Among the first was Hoppy the Marvel Bunny, originally published by Fawcett Comics in 1942. With elements borrowed from Fawcett's popular Captain Marvel (later called Shazam), Hoppy is a pink rabbit who shouts "Shazam!" to access his superpowers.

Another heroic leporine, Super Rabbit, made his 1943 debut in Timely Comics, a predecessor to Marvel Comics. In the comic, Super Rabbit, the alter ego of Waffles Bunny, is a powerfully built rabbit able to fly. The 1940s represented the golden age of comic books, and decades would pass before additional rabbit heroes emerged, such as Captain Carrot (1982), Cutey Bunny (1982), Thunderbunny (1984), and Bucky O'Hare (1991). In 1984, Thoughts and Images Comics released its first comic to include the rabbit character Miyamoto Usagi (*usagi* is Japanese for rabbit), created by Stan Sakai. Three years later, Usagi became a main character and was featured in the Usagi Yojimbo series, in which he is a sword-touting rōnin during the Edo period of Japan (1603–1867), wandering the land and occasionally offering his services as a bodyguard. The stories are heavily influenced by Japanese history and folklore.

A cartoon rabbit doesn't require an entire comic book to have an impact, however—sometimes just a few panels in a newspaper will do. Such was the case with Frisky the Rabbit, a character created by author and illustrator Nan Fullarton in 1948. We don't hear much about Frisky these days, but in the 1950s, he made a big impression. To fully appreciate the character's influence, two pieces of information are essential: first, he had an entirely Australian pedigree, and second, the height of his fame coincided with (or was due to) Australia's release of a lethal disease called myxomatosis to control its ever-growing wild rabbit population. Adding another layer of context to this is the ongoing rhetoric articulated to the nation's children that, as environmental scholar Kate Wright puts it, "rabbit love is inappropriate because it conflicts with ecological politics."

This narrative was absolutely at odds with Fullarton, an Australian native who confessed to a "wholehearted admiration for our rabbits." She later said she made a rabbit the star of her comic strip because "a rabbit was about as Australian as you could get at that time" and described Frisky as "a sturdy, kindly little person full of initiative and resource, utterly reliable in a crisis." Such qualities served Frisky well in his playful exploits, which appeared in the comics supplement of *The Sunday Herald* and in the 1956 book *The Adventures of Frisky: A Story of the Australian Bush*. But things took a serious turn in September of 1953, when Frisky sailed the country's longest river, the Murray, and collapsed after being bitten by a mosquito carrying the deadly myxoma virus. Fortunately, an obliging pelican carried Frisky in his beak to an animal sanctuary, where a staff member gave the ailing bunny a vaccine. Concerned readers—many of whom sent letters to the paper—hoped for the best, and several anxious Sundays later, Frisky was out of bed and as lively as ever.

Not everyone was happy about this storyline, least of all Australia's farmers, who saw (and still see) rabbits as a threat to local crops and produce. Even the English biologist Julian Huxley, one of the founders of the World Wildlife Fund, expressed dismay over the attention Frisky was receiving. "The most peculiar thing I have seen in Australia is a comic strip in the *Sunday Herald* which has a rabbit recovering from myxomatosis as its hero," he said just before departing the country. Frisky had his defenders of course, even in the national press. After disparaging the celebration of what many considered an agricultural nuisance, a columnist for *The Sun-Herald* had to acknowledge that "Miss Nan Fullarton's Frisky would poll well in any election." Still others were more to the point. As a correspondent for *The Sydney Morning Herald* wrote shortly after Frisky had recuperated, "Rabbits must be one of the most likable pests ever to afflict a country."

In 1979, a very different sort of rabbit protagonist made his debut with the publication of *Bunnicula: A Rabbit Tale of Mystery*. The mostly humorous story aimed at young readers is told from the viewpoint of a dog named Harold, who shares a home with Mr. and Mrs. Monroe, their two sons, one cat, and a black-and-white rabbit the family has named Bunnicula because they found him in a movie theater that was showing *Dracula*. Bunnicula may or may not be sucking the household vegetables dry. That he has fangs and a widow's peak like Eddie Munster should be tremendous clues, but only Chester the cat is suspicious, and he tries to enlist Harold in efforts to expose the ravenous rabbit.

Bunnicula was created by wife and husband Deborah and James Howe, two underemployed actors-turned-writers who were inspired by the old vampire movies they would watch together on late-night television. Fans of satire, the couple decided that a rabbit would be the least likely vampire anyone could imagine, but a bunny sinking his teeth into human necks seemed a little too implausible. "Besides," James Howe later recalled, "logic told us that if there were such a thing as a vampire rabbit, he would most likely be a vegetarian. And so Bunnicula's victims became carrots and tomatoes and, in one of my favorite scenes in the book, a poor, unsuspecting zucchini!" The novel became a bona fide hit, spawning not only six sequels (so far) but also a TV special, an animated series, toys, and even a musical adaptation.

Some books, like *Bunnicula*, are read and enjoyed, perhaps more than once. Other stories are absorbed into our consciousness in a way that can help shape who we are, enhancing their pop-culture status. *The Velveteen Rabbit: Or How Toys Become Real* by Margery Williams is that sort of story. Published in 1922, *The Velveteen Rabbit* is ostensibly a children's book about a young boy who receives a toy rabbit one Christmas. The Boy enjoys the Rabbit for a couple of hours before he's distracted and playing with other, more interesting toys. Soon the sawdust-stuffed Rabbit is forgotten, relegated to a cupboard in the nursery where other overlooked toys reside. One such toy, the Skin Horse, has been there the longest, and he tells the Rabbit about the magic of being made Real. When a child loves you for a very long time, he says—not only as a plaything but *really* loves you—then you become Real.

The Rabbit longs to become Real, and one day he's plucked from the nursery to sleep with the Boy. The Boy spends many nights with the Rabbit, holding him tightly, talking to him, and eventually hugging off some of his velveteen fur and kissing away some of the pink from his nose. He plays with him during the day, as well: picnics in the grass, rides in the wheelbarrow, and adventures in the garden. When the Boy tells his nanny that the Rabbit isn't a toy, he's *real*, the Rabbit is overjoyed and begins to think of himself that way, too. As weeks pass, the Boy's love rubs the Rabbit's thread whiskers off and he loses his shape; to the Boy, however, he is as beautiful as ever.

Dramatic changes occur when the Boy is bedridden with scarlet fever and his room is to be disinfected. The doctor orders that all the germ-covered books and toys the Boy played with must be destroyed, including his beloved Rabbit. That night, tossed into a sack and left in the garden to be burned, the Rabbit sheds a tear and thus begins his metamorphosis into a real rabbit—not a toy rabbit who is *considered* Real because he is loved but one magically reborn as an actual rabbit who will enjoy life in "Rabbit-land" with other rabbits "for ever and ever." It's easy to see these events as part of a simple fable, but they also echo the story of Easter, with the Rabbit being sacrificed so that someone else (the Boy) might be saved; he is resurrected and takes his place in some version of heaven. And let's not forget that the Rabbit came to the Boy on Christmas.

In the final poignant scene, several seasons have passed, and the now-healthy Boy comes to the woods to play. Here Rabbit-land is also the woods in real life, and the Boy gets close enough to see the Rabbit. The Rabbit knows the Boy, but there isn't even a glimmer of recognition in the Boy's eyes—he sees only an animal who looks a bit like his long-lost toy Rabbit. To the Rabbit, however, here is the Boy whose love helped him become Real. There will be no reunion for these two friends who once shared so much. It's a tear-jerking moment, to be sure. "The truth is," novelist David Foster Wallace said, "I don't think I've ever found anything as purely 'moving' as the end of *The Velveteen Rabbit* when I first read it."

The Velveteen Rabbit is filled with many significant themes: friendship, empathy, innocence, loss, kindness, authenticity, unconditional love. Not exactly your typical children's story. Perhaps that's why some critics don't care for it. In her review in *The New Yorker*, for instance, Faith McNulty wrote, "The book gives no hint that there is any way to meet the tragedy of lost love and betrayal other than letting the heart break." I think such criticism misses the story's central premise, which is that love isn't diminished by change but transcends it. This is possible because, as sociologist Allan Kellehear puts it, "both children and their toys live on as memories and dreams, the past a living social presence and influence on the present." The Boy may not recognize the Rabbit he once knew but will long remember him, and the Rabbit—perhaps being made of sterner stuffing—will *always* remember the Boy.

To say rabbits have made their mark on popular culture is like saying Mozart had a penchant for music. Indeed, rabbits are more *en vogue* today than ever, and you'll find this reflected not just in movies and the sales of children's toys, books, cereal, and comic books but also on packaging for pastas, soups, wines, and beers. Rabbits grace greeting cards, stationery, calendars, and wrapping paper. They appear on jewelry, T-shirts, baseball caps, purses, neck ties, scarves, socks, dresses, sweaters, wallets, slippers, and umbrellas as well as spoons, forks, and chopsticks. If that's not enough to satisfy you, they also adorn dinner plates, tea towels, measuring cups, kitchen aprons, and door mats. You can convert your bedroom into a lagomorph-themed retreat with blankets, bed sheets, rugs, wallpaper, curtains, dresser, lamps, and an alarm clock all festooned with rabbits. Your bathroom can be a rabbit haven as well, with shower curtains, bath soaps and soap holders, lotion dispensers, bath towels, bathmats, toothbrushes, toothbrush holders, and mirrors made in the image of bunnies. You can even sit on a rabbit toilet seat, although I am not entirely sure why you'd want to. And all these are designed for adults, not children. You can buy a cake pan or a cookie jar shaped like a rabbit or a coffee mug reading "Bunny Person." In fact, the entire rabbit coffee mug business is an industry all its own, and you can enjoy your morning joe or tea in a ceramic cup fashioned like a bunny, enlivened with bunny wisdom ("Alice: How long is forever? White Rabbit: Sometimes, just one second"), or showcasing the bunny character of your choice. It's not your imagination ... bunnies are everywhere.

The rabbit's high profile in pop culture represents not just the public's love of furry and playful critters but also the appeal of rabbits as animals who are thoroughly present. They remind us to be our best selves, detached from the exterior world while remaining engaged with others. If all this sentiment sounds a little too philosophical to be attributed to the humble rabbit, think for a moment what lagomorphs have come to symbolize— rebirth, balance, rejuvenation, speed, awareness, resurrection, fertility, spring, purity, resourcefulness, abundance, creativity, magic, harmony—and then consider how many of these are life-affirming qualities or at least characteristics that bring deep meaning to our existence. Such attributes have made the simple act of wearing a Peter Rabbit T-shirt, hugging a toy Thumper, or getting a rabbit tattoo a celebration of everything these animals embody.

Chapter Seven

Lagomorphs in History

With a finer understanding of Napoleonic strategy than most of his generals, the rabbit horde divided into two wings and poured round the flanks of the party and headed for the Imperial Coach.
—David Chandler, *The Campaigns of Napoleon*

Rabbits occupy such a distinctive place in our collective consciousness—subjects of literature and lore, muses to artists and authors, stars of screens large and small—that it can be easy to forget we are also talking about a living, breathing animal. But there are occasions when they remind us of their reality, transcending whatever pop-culture symbolism they may represent to help define a moment in history, even when they remain anonymous to us. One such moment occurred on Friday, April 20, 1979, when Jimmy Carter, the thirty-ninth president of the United States, was taking some time off from his reelection campaign and enjoying the last full day of his vacation. He got into a little boat on a small pond near his home in Plains, Georgia, and paddled out to do some fishing. Carter suddenly noticed he wasn't alone on the pond: heading his way, and making good time, was some kind of furry woodland critter. When he saw it was a rabbit swimming toward him, Carter used his paddle to splash water in the animal's direction, and the bunny swam back toward shore.

And that likely would have been the end of the episode had the president not mentioned it to his press secretary, who then shared it with an Associated Press reporter. Soon national newspapers including *The Washington Post* and *The New York Times* were covering the story, which was embellished so much that the incident took on the magnitude of an all-out amphibious assault, with the rabbit supposedly flaring their nostrils, hissing, gnashing their teeth, and trying to board Carter's boat with nefarious intentions. Many people, even among his own staff, thought the president was a liar, believing—erroneously— that no rabbit can swim. Meanwhile, political cartoonists had great fun with the event: one cartoon spoofed the marketing of a certain shark-themed blockbuster by showing a giant, buck-toothed bunny swimming beneath Carter in a canoe with the illustration headlined "PAWS."

A White House photographer positioned on a bluff overlooking the pond had captured the encounter on film, and the photo proved there was indeed a rabbit swimming near the president. Much to Carter's dismay, this only fanned the flames of what became known as the "killer rabbit" affair (this was just four years after the release of *Monty Python and the Holy Grail* with its Killer Rabbit of Caerbannog). The mammal at the center of this news story was most likely a swamp rabbit (*Sylvilagus aquaticus*), a species perfectly at home wading into water. President Carter told reporters two months after the incident that he didn't believe the animal meant him any harm. "My guess is that the rabbit had been startled by some dogs or something and had jumped in the pond and was just looking for a dry place to crawl," he said. Overall, the confrontation made the beleaguered commander-in-chief look weak, perhaps exacerbated by the fact that he was the first president since Herbert Hoover not to bomb anyone.

While a swamp rabbit may enjoy the occasional swim, most leporines will go to great lengths to avoid dampening their fur. Hares living in the rapidly growing environs of eighteenth- and nineteenth-century Saint Petersburg, Russia, frequently found themselves running for high ground, thanks to floods that routinely overwhelmed parts of the city. Saint Petersburg was built on drained marshland, so flooding was hardly a surprise. During one such flood, the city's founder, Tsar Peter I, otherwise known as Peter the Great, had just landed his boat on a small island in the Neva River and was stepping ashore when a clever hare is said to have hopped into one of his spacious boots to escape the rising water. This story is so well loved that the city commissioned a metal statue in the hare's honor. Unveiled in 2003, the 300th anniversary of Saint Petersburg's founding, *The Hare Escaping Flooding* stands about 2 feet (0.6 m) tall and is mounted atop a wooden piling in the river beside Zayachy Ostrov—or "Hare Island."

A century after Peter the Great, another leader would have an historic lagomorph encounter. It was July of 1807, and Napoleon Bonaparte of France had just made peace with Russia, ending a war and leaving him in command of most of western and central Europe. In the mood to celebrate, Napoleon ordered his chief of staff, Louis-Alexandre Berthier, to collect rabbits for a hunt. On the appointed morning, Napoleon and his convoy arrived at the field just outside of Paris and prepared for the shoot. But when the rabbits were released from their cages, they did not run for cover as expected. Instead, like French revolutionaries storming the Bastille, hundreds—some historians say thousands—of rabbits raced toward Napoleon and his entourage. Nervous laughter soon gave way to alarm as a veritable bunny blitz overwhelmed the imperial guards and swarmed the emperor himself. They climbed his trousers and chased him back to his carriage, into which some rabbits reportedly followed him. Looking for a cause behind what he considered an embarrassing defeat, Napoleon learned that rather than catching wild rabbits, Berthier had purchased bunnies from a breeder. These tame animals were accustomed to being fed regularly by a farmer bearing delicious foodstuffs but likely hadn't had anything to eat for a day or two. Upon being set free, the hungry horde naturally made a beeline for the emperor and his men.

Napoleon's retreat from the bunny brigade shares some details with another event that came to light in the same year. In his 1807 book *Travels in Scotland by an Unusual Route*, Reverend James Hall describes his conversation with a man at a Scottish inn in the town of Cupar, near the North Sea coast. The man, he writes, tells the author about meeting a rabbit breeder the day before who was transporting a hundred of the animals to the West Highlands. The breeder rented a room for the night, placing the rabbits inside and tossing them a supply of greens before heading off to bed. The gentleman in Rev. Hall's story happened to rent the room beside the breeder's, and sometime during the evening a gust of wind blew open the adjoining door, at which point a hundred rabbits came rushing in and quickly besieged his bed. The gentleman reports how the rabbits ran over his head, face, and arms and that some even sought shelter beneath the blankets. Apparently not a fan of the furry creatures, he screamed for help, but none arrived. "Thinking himself surrounded by a thousand devils, which he found before, behind, and round about him, he, at length, found the door and ran down stairs naked in the dark," writes Hall. The rabbits were just as afraid of the shrieking, naked man and also headed out the door and down the stairs, and soon "the whole house was in an uproar." It seems it took some time for the breeder to finally locate all the rabbits, who had secreted themselves in a wide range of hiding places.

It doesn't happen often, it must be said, but once in a great while a rabbit becomes part of history by way of some criminal enterprise. The felonious activity of one eighteenth-century highway robber, for instance—described in the press as "an impudent fellow"—involved stepping up to a coach on an English country road with a rabbit in one hand and a pistol in the other and saying, "By

God, gentlemen, you must and shall buy this rabbit!" The media did not report how successful this tactic was.

Rabbits can bring out the softer side of even the most hardened outlaw, and in the 1930s, no two fugitives were as notorious as Clyde Barrow and Bonnie Parker. While the young bandits robbed and shot their way across the central United States and kept one step ahead of police in 1934, they paused long enough for Bonnie to buy a white rabbit she named Sonny Boy, who was to be an Easter gift for her mother in Dallas. Until they could deliver Sonny Boy, he lived in the back seat of the couple's stolen Ford sedan, which was strewn with lettuce and carrots. Occasionally they would pull over on a rural lane and let Sonny Boy out to stretch his legs and graze on grass. On April 18, Bonnie and Clyde cautiously arranged a rendezvous with their families in Texas, and Bonnie handed Sonny Boy over to her mother. "Keep him away from the cops," she said. "He's been in two gun battles and he'll land at Huntsville [Prison] if the law finds it out."

While it's tempting to think of rabbits as being more bashful than bold, a review of history reveals countless examples of these animals rescuing people from a variety of calamitous circumstances. The Castello family of Lezignan, France, had their rabbits to thank for their very lives when their house caught fire late one night in 1912. The rabbits' squealing woke Mr. Castello, who thought he was hearing burglars, and he ran downstairs to find that a candle he'd left burning had set the curtains on fire. "Owing to the warning of the rabbits Castello was able to save his wife and four children, and the rabbits themselves," reads one newspaper account, which adds that soon after, the dwelling's roof fell in. In a similar fashion, it was the cries of a house rabbit that saved the Colen family — father, mother, child, and the rabbit — from their burning home in Hazel Park, Michigan, in 1932. Likewise, in 1951, neighbors heard the squeals of a companion rabbit in the burning home of Charles Leneau, a resident of Braintree, Massachusetts, and thought it was the Leneau baby crying. They rushed over, helped extinguish the blaze, and everyone was safe.

In 1984, a gray-and-white dwarf bunny named Radar smelled smoke inside a duplex in Toledo, Ohio, and scratched at a door, waking Bruce Works and his fiancée, Gail Christofferson, who rushed their hero outside in a portable cooler. Scratching on a door also helped a bun named Rabbit rescue his human companions, Gerry and Michelle Finn of Sydney, Australia. It was 2008, and the Finns awoke to find flames devouring their house, so they wisely grabbed their furry friend and got out. The whole ordeal left the Finns shaken, though Rabbit seems to have weathered it well. "He's just sort of an inside pet," said Mrs. Finn, "but I don't think he was very impressed."

The sound of two bunnies thumping saved a family from fire in 2013. Alex and Nicole Ochotorena, of Tucson, Arizona, and five of their six children were snug in their beds at 3:30 a.m. when out in the kitchen rabbits Bun Bun and Promise began drumming with their hindlegs. Checking to see what the late-night commotion was all about, Nicole found the slow cooker going up in flames. She quickly woke Alex, and everyone got out safely. None of the home's smoke alarms had sounded. "My bunnies are my lifesavers," Nicole told a reporter. "They saved my life and they saved my kids."

Not all of these stories involve companion rabbits. In 1960, kindhearted Josef Frischauf and his equally compassionate wife found a wild rabbit with an injured foot near their home in Vienna, Austria. They brought the rabbit inside, applied whatever first aid they could, and placed their little patient in a soft bed in their bedroom. Early one morning soon after, a fire broke out in the house. Fortunately for all involved, the rabbit's foot had healed well enough for him to loudly thump, raising the alarm. The Frischaufs escaped with the bunny, who ran off into the woods, presumably much happier to be back in nature.

Nor do all of these rescues involve fires. Just ask Blazer, a white-and-brown Lop who at 2:30 a.m. on November 16, 2013, smelled a gas leak in the home she shared with Jake and Mary Pruett in Bridgeton, New Jersey. Blazer climbed the small stairs that gave her access to the couple's bed and made honking noises, rousing Mary from sleep. (She also walked on Mary's face, just to be sure she'd wake up.) Smelling the gas, Mary woke her husband, and they quickly left the house with Blazer.

Then there's Dory, who in 2004 jumped onto the chest of Simon Steggall after he had slumped into a diabetic coma in Cambridgeshire, England. The 7-pound (3-kg) rabbit thumped with her hindlegs and used her forepaws to "dig" at his torso, which caught the attention of Simon's wife, Victoria, who called paramedics. "Victoria told me later that Dory had made a terrible fuss, seeming very upset," said Simon. "She kept pawing at me, like she was trying to wake me up, until Victoria came over to see what was wrong." He realizes that Dory saved his life. "I knew right away that if she hadn't acted the way she did, I could easily have died." For her life-saving actions, Dory was made the first-ever honorary animal member of the Rabbit Welfare Association, the UK's largest organization for rabbit lovers.

The year following Dory's heroism, a rabbit in the United States named Robin also made a name for herself. Robin slept in a cage next to the bedroom of Ed and Darcy Murphy of Port Bryon, Illinois. One morning at about 3:00, Ed, who is a very sound sleeper, awoke to the sound of Robin making a tremendous commotion. "She was going wild," he said. "It wasn't like her at all." Ed checked on the bunny but saw nothing wrong. Then he noticed Darcy was making noises like she was having a bad dream—but her eyes were wide open. "She was staring straight ahead," said Ed, who immediately called 911 and then grabbed some cake frosting from the kitchen because his pregnant wife had gestational diabetes; they kept frosting in case her blood sugar got too low. Darcy spent five days in the hospital, but she and her baby were fine. Dr. Anita Pinc, her obstetrician, explained that Darcy had gone into shock from receiving too much insulin. "I guess the rabbit was telling her husband 'Wake up, wake up. Something is wrong with your wife,'" she said. "It was very good the rabbit woke them up and saved her life." An animal behaviorist at Texas A&M University, Dr. Bonnie Beaver, speculates that Robin could sense the ketone odors Darcy's body was producing. Whatever caused the bunny to raise the alarm, says Darcy, "Robin was the reason that everything worked out the way it did."

GOAL!
It was 1960, and a soccer match in Belgrade, Serbia, between Gradac and Baljak was in the final moments, the score 0–0, when a rabbit suddenly darted onto the field and knocked the ball past the Gradac team's goalkeeper and into the net. The referee awarded the goal, and the rabbit won the game for Baljak.

A story from 1875 credits a wild rabbit with saving the life of a man named Clyde, who found himself buried in a Montana silver mine after the roof of a mineshaft caved in. "There was nothing I could do to release myself," he recalled. "I knew that if relief did not come from the outside I must perish. No one knew I had gone there." Although there was a road near the mine, it was not frequently traveled, and day after day Clyde's shouts for help brought no one. "The morning of my fourth day of imprisonment I heard something crawl into my grave. I lighted my candle and saw a rabbit." Acting quickly, Clyde tore strips of his shirt to create a halter, attached some fishing line, extended the length with his watch chain, and managed to get the halter over the rabbit's head. Then he scribbled a few lines describing his condition on paper from his diary, fastened the note to the far end of the line, and released his long-eared messenger. "About three hours afterwards I felt the line pulled; then someone called." It took about nine hours to free Clyde from the mine, after which the rabbit was hailed as a hero, fed an assortment of leporine delicacies, and liberated. "A rabbit saved my life," Clyde later told a friend, and he swore never to harm one.

Other times, rabbits play a significant role in providing comfort and encouragement in life-threatening situations. On June 1, 1919, soldiers with the 25th Engineers Regiment who had served in France were returning to San Francisco from the East Coast on the Western Pacific Railroad when five cars of the train slid into Salt Creek in southeastern Nebraska while most of them slept. The creek, swollen from a rainstorm, completely covered one car, and many men woke up underwater. Among them was Corporal Chester Kinnear, who had been sleeping in a lower berth. "The car was settling down further into the creek when I reached up to pull myself out by main force," he said. That's when Cpl. Kinnear stuck his hand through a broken window and felt a rabbit crouching between two railroad ties. He credited the animal with saving his life. "I finally yanked myself loose from the frame and I'm taking bunny home to Oakland. A fellow in one of the other cars gave me and bunny a blanket, and that's all the clothes we have between us." While I would never endorse taking a healthy animal home from the wild, in addition to the kinship between them born of a shared near-death experience, perhaps Cpl. Kinnear felt the rabbit needed medical attention.

And even though I'd also never approve of putting an animal in harm's way, I would be remiss if I didn't share the stories of two rabbits who lived aboard ships during World War II. Many sailors and soldiers kept animals as morale-boosting mascots during the war, but few seemed to have the extraordinary ability of a rabbit named Handy Built to sense when a battle was about to commence. Handy lived on the HMCS *Haida*, a destroyer that served the Royal Canadian Navy. "He once woke me up even before action stations were sounded," said Able Seaman John McGregor, who looked after the brown-and-white Dutch. "I woke up some of the other fellows and they were at their guns faster than would have been possible without Handy's warning." Because of the dangers of being on board the ship, Handy often stayed in a cage, but he could be found on the upper deck, enjoying the sunshine with the crew. After the war, Handy Built was adopted by Captain Harry de Wolfe, commander of the *Haida*, and spent the remainder of his days in the comparative safety and comfort of civilian life in Halifax, Nova Scotia. The British Humane Society decorated him with a distinguished service medal for bravery.

Acting as a mascot on another warship was Midway, a young bunny brought onboard the aircraft carrier USS *Yorktown* in Honolulu by Navy cook Thomas L. J. Saxon. The *Yorktown* was torpedoed during the Battle of Midway on June 4, 1942, so Saxon had to react quickly to save his furry friend. "When we start to abandon ship," he said, "I still have her with me and I take my gas mask out and throw the thing away." He then put Midway in the bag and jumped overboard with her, hurting his back in the process. "I am so busy getting her off the ship I leave all my money behind in my locker." A US destroyer eventually rescued Saxon and Midway, and Navy doctors treated them both for exposure. When the pair reached port in San Francisco seven weeks later and Saxon told their story, reporters and the public, hungry for good news, ate it up.

Photos of the 23-year-old sailor, bearded and smiling, and Midway, her head peeking out of the gas mask bag on his lap, made newspapers across the country. Saxon was soon stationed at California's Naval Air Station Alameda amid Midway's growing celebrity. But the injury to his back put him in the hospital, so Midway was temporarily adopted by an officer of the Alameda police department. Sadly, Saxon died of his injuries in 1943, and his friends had Midway delivered to his home in Foxworth, Mississippi, where his widow, Marie, found her a mate named Red. Midway passed away in December of 1947.

Although rabbits do not feature in news stories as frequently as some other animals, when they do appear, it's often because they are so misunderstood. This was especially true in the nineteenth and early twentieth centuries, when rabbits were quickly becoming a favorite companion animal for both children and adults. After a Mrs. J. E. Band was seen leading a white Angora rabbit named Bunny by a ribbon around parks in Washington, DC, in 1911, Reverend Charles Pate, pastor of a local church, said her actions were "indescribably silly." He went on to rail against the "fad" of having rabbits as companions, warning that the practice leads to neglected children and divorce. *The Washington Times* published Mrs. Band's response, in which she pointed out that domestic strife could certainly be caused by less important issues than having an animal in the home. "These little pets were made by the same Divine hand that made man and woman," she reminded the reverend. "I'm sure God did not think he made anything worthless."

The Unicorn Rabbit

Nineteenth-century California is the setting for many tall tales about animals, from yellow dogs to jumping frogs. But at least one remarkable animal was genuine: the unicorn rabbit of Tocaloma. In this tiny town in Marin County, Joseph Bertrand built a grand, three-story hotel that catered to many guests over the years, perhaps none so beloved as a certain cotton-tailed rabbit who appeared outside the door one day. He was just like any other rabbit, except for having an unusual genetic mutation: a single long ear that faced backward directly on top of his head. Someone at the Bertrand Hotel dubbed him the "unicorn rabbit," and Bertrand's daughter adopted him. According to one 1896 newspaper account, "He hops about the hotel as contented as any rabbit could be, and when picked up and petted seems to be delighted at receiving the attention."

At about the same time that Mrs. Band and Bunny were causing a stir in the USA, on the other side of the Atlantic Lady Lelia Samuelson was making headlines with her rabbit Benjamin. Dubbed by reporters "the bunny with brains," Benjamin became famous for following Lady Samuelson wherever she went and for performing tricks that seemed to amaze rabbit guardians in 1910, such as coming when he heard his name and standing on his hindlegs to request a treat. That Benjamin was given media attention probably had more to do with his exclusive address at Hatchford Park, Surrey, than with his mental prowess, since his clever behavior was and is pretty standard for rabbits. Still, his conduct apparently surprised Lady Samuelson as much as it did the public, many of whom came to the house to witness Benjamin's antics, which also included chasing dogs and eating virtually anything made of paper. "His 'manageress,' Miss Le Duix, narrowly averted a tragedy a few weeks ago, just arriving in time to prevent him from devouring a £5 note," reported *The New Zealand Herald*. Attempting to explain Benjamin's intelligence, Lady Samuelson observed that from birth he "was no ordinary rabbit and must have inherited exceptional qualities from his parents. His father was a Belgian hare, and his mother an English silver-grey." If only Benjamin could have taught his human companions not to feed him tea, cookies, and tobacco, the latter of which he would eat from cigarettes.

A rabbit named Wilfred made international news and enjoyed a bit of royal attention in 1926, when King George V was staying in Yorkshire, England. The monarch's hosts, the Duke and Duchess of Devonshire, told him about a very sick young girl, Kathleen Tomlinson, who was the daughter of the rector of nearby Bolton Abbey. Hoping to cheer her up, King George arranged to visit her, and when she was brought into Bolton Hall in a wheelchair, she carried little Wilfred in her arms. Kathleen tearfully mentioned that her brother Robert shared custody of Wilfred, but he intended to sell him to a friend in the village. "What a shame," replied the king, who promptly offered to pay the boy for his share in Wilfred. "He's worth five shillings," Robert said, upon which the king's representative paid him ten and then notified six-year-old Kathleen that she was henceforth the rabbit's sole guardian. When Wilfred died in 1927, the king sent a wreath of flowers to be laid on the grave, which was in a corner of the Tomlinsons' garden. (Incidentally, Princess Mary, the king's only daughter, reportedly favored rabbits as pets and kept a number of them at York Cottage, the royal house at Sandringham, in the 1920s, as did the king's granddaughters, Princess Elizabeth—the future queen—and Princess Margaret, in the late 1930s. In the 1950s, the favorite companion animal of Prince Charles, son of Queen Elizabeth, was said to be his rabbit Harvey.)

Because rabbits are generally docile and easy to carry about, people have been only too happy to bring them on errands or even vacations, and in the nineteenth century the results could sometimes be either educational or frustrating. An article from an 1875 edition of England's *Shields Gazette and Daily Telegraph* reported on a rabbit named Joe, whose guardian brought him into the city to have their friendship commemorated with a photograph. Early cameras had very slow shutter speeds, which required the subjects to hold quite still. The guardian recalls:

When the photographer heard that he was required to take the photograph of a rabbit, he declared it was impossible, and he didn't see how it was to be done. Then he quoted the anecdote of a lady who wished to have her cat done.

When the job was nearly finished, the cat sprang up the wall. I assured him that Joe would not jump up the wall. So he began to work. I sat down and took Joe on my knee. He behaved so well, that when it was done, the man said, "If any one moved, it was you." The idea of taking Joe's photograph was so novel, that the people did not know what price to charge, and in the end did not charge for Joe at all.

Consider, too, the British family who went on holiday with their rabbit in 1893. In a letter to the editor of the *London Evening Standard*, the father describes their vexing experiences riding an Italian train with their bunny:

Early in the month, along with my wife and two children, I travelled by rail from Turin to Genoa. The fare of each was fifteen francs, and the same for baggage. My youngest child, aged thirteen, had a small pet rabbit, which she carried in a basket. *En route* the ticket collector happened to come to the door and espied it, and at once demanded twelve francs for its transport.

The father considered such a fee extortion, and he refused to pay. Upon arriving at their destination, however, he was confronted by the station officials, who ridiculed the man by forcing him to forfeit the sum of 11 francs and 60 centimes for transporting the rabbit—and another 30 centimes in taxes.

Speed Racer

Hares are notoriously fast, as witnessed firsthand by spectators at an auto race in San Diego, California, in 1933. Racecar driver Earl Manselle had just turned onto the straightaway and was pulling ahead when a jackrabbit loped onto the track in front him and nine other speeding cars. As Manselle stepped on the gas, the

**hare, according to a news report, "laid back its ears and
had a lead of several car lengths passing the grandstand,"
then veered off onto the infield to rest. Manselle said he
was driving more than 65 miles an hour (104.6 km/h).**

Managing much better in their travels were a white Angora
named Sniffy and her guardians, Kathryn and Leo Watts of
Calexico, California. Kathryn was the principal of an elementary
school, and Sniffy had been a gift to her from some of the
students in 1936. Apparently, Kathryn was able to take plenty of
time off work, as she and her husband managed to bring Sniffy
with them to (then) all 48 states in the USA, as well as to Canada
and Mexico. Sniffy quickly gained national attention not just for
riding in the front seat of the car but also for staying in fancy
hotel rooms. In 1939, they traveled to New Jersey to appear on
the radio program *Famous First Facts*, hosted by Joseph Nathan
Kane. Leo had pitched Sniffy as a guest to the show's producers,
telling them that she was the first rabbit to become a household
pet and the first rabbit to be led on a leash. Whether or not
he truly believed either of these wildly erroneous assertions is
unknown, but the producers invited Sniffy to appear on their
April 6 broadcast, capitalizing on the upcoming Easter holiday.
Described on the show as "the world's most widely-traveled
rabbit," Sniffy remained characteristically quiet in the studio
while Kathryn managed to slip in a few on-air promotions for
the excellent produce grown in the Imperial Valley around their
hometown (Sniffy was said to be a fan of the carrots and lettuce).
They then made their way to Washington, DC, where Sniffy was
a big hit at the White House and its Easter Monday festival for
children. The well-traveled rabbit died in her sleep following an
illness in 1944 at eight years and two months of age.

Of all the rabbit-related stories covered in the news or found in
the pages of history books, perhaps my favorite demonstrates

the promising implications for human–animal relationships. It was the spring of 2003, and a shipment of flowers from the Netherlands had just arrived at a florist shop in Cromer, England, about 140 miles (225 km) northeast of London. When shop owner Helen Parriss opened the box, there among the chrysanthemums was a wild female rabbit who had miraculously survived the six-day journey across the North Sea. "I like anything furry," says Helen, "so we just took her out and started cuddling her. She was so cute. Then we made a little nest in a box for her." Helen contacted the RSPCA, and soon the UK's Department for Environment, Food, and Rural Affairs phoned her to say that the little stowaway faced euthanasia unless she was willing to have her put into quarantine for six months and foot the bill, which would amount to £700 (the equivalent of about US$1120 at the time). "We thought, 'Blimey!'" she says with a laugh.

Helen named the seven-week-old bunny Spot for the little white dot on her forehead (a common marking on young wild rabbits) and was determined to help her. She launched the Save Our Spot campaign and was thrilled with the response. "Because I have had businesses for a long time, there were a lot of local people who knew me, and then lots of people read about it in the national newspapers." The public became captivated by the rabbit refugee and happily sent in donations from across the country. Meanwhile, local merchants set up "bunny boxes" at their stores for customers to contribute to the effort. Contributions at Ottakar's bookshop in Norwich, for instance, brought in £150. Instructors in Essex classrooms even used Spot's story to help foreign students learning English with reading and comprehension.

With more than enough money collected to cover Spot's half a year with animal control officials in the neighboring county of Cambridgeshire, Helen began planning how to help her once she was released. She'd had companion rabbits as a child, and her initial hope was to keep Spot. "She is wild," she told a reporter in 2003, "but we were told she might be able to become a pet if she was kept in the house." Since the Parriss family already lived with a dog, they decided it would be better to find Spot a home in one of England's many sanctuaries. "It needed to be somewhere where she gets a decent amount of space and which is completely safe." After contacting more than 40 animal rescue centers, Helen settled on Hillside Animal Sanctuary, which was not far from her shop. She also appreciated sanctuary founder Wendy Valentine's compassion. "She's very much an activist for kindness to animals," she says, adding that all the excess donations were given to Hillside. Upon her release from quarantine, Spot was followed by a television news crew as she was welcomed into the sanctuary's population of rescued rabbits. "She went on to live a long and happy rabbit life at Hillside," says Wendy, "and we lost her in 2010."

What I find so appealing about this story is that one person's chance encounter with an animal impacted so many other lives, most of whom would never meet Spot, and eventually led to this single rabbit becoming an ambassador for her species. Countless people learned about not just Spot but also rabbits in general and the threats they face. Some two decades later, Helen, who now owns a jewelry store, seems quite pleased with her role in the events and believes anyone in her place would do the same thing, with similar results. "With all that goes on in this world, I think people are as passionate about saving animals as anything else," she says. "You get some nasty people as well, but you get some incredibly kind people."

Chapter Eight

Bunny Biology

In the twilight and the night the rabbits came regularly and made a hearty meal.
—Henry David Thoreau, *Walden*

If you are lucky, you might observe a wild rabbit in their element. To do so, you will need to spend some very quiet time in nature at dawn or dusk, when these crepuscular animals are most active, because sunrise and sunset present the safest moments for them to emerge from their burrows to graze and socialize. In the twilight, nocturnal (nighttime) predators have trouble seeing because the light is too bright, and diurnal (daytime) predators have trouble seeing because the light is too dim, giving bunnies a little extra protection.

Ironically, a rabbit's eyesight isn't their greatest asset. Even though they have nearly 360-degree, panoramic vision—thanks to slightly protruding eyes placed on either side of their head— rabbits have two blind spots: one is an area about 10 degrees wide below their chin and the other is directly behind their head. They are also farsighted, which helps them spot predators such as hawks from a long distance but means they may not be able to focus on objects near them.

Not all experts agree on the full mechanics of a rabbit's vision (just as we may never know exactly what a bunny is thinking), but we can say that in comparison with some other animals, rabbits have large eyes, which gather more light and may help them see better in low-light conditions. Moreover, it is likely that most of what rabbits are looking at is seen in two dimensions. There is, however, an area that they see when looking forward in which the field of view from the left eye and the field of view from the right eye overlap, giving them a binocular zone of approximately 24 percent; in this intersecting field they have depth perception and see in three dimensions, just like primates, felines, owls, and other animals with front-facing eyes.

Rabbits compensate for their inability to perceive the relative distance of objects in their remaining field of view by moving their head up and down or side to side, creating visual cues through what is known as a motion parallax. You can see how the motion parallax phenomenon works when riding in a vehicle or train—you'll notice that nearby trees and buildings sweep past faster than mountains or other landmarks far away. By shifting the perspective (through their head movement) and changing the apparent position of an object, rabbits essentially use a kind of intuitive geometry to calculate its distance. (Other animals with laterally placed eyes, such as pigeons and bees, do this too.)

They also apparently have a limited ability to see color, although rabbits can distinguish blue and green, says Dr. David Williams, who teaches veterinary ophthalmology at the University of Cambridge. "I particularly like the way that the rabbit's ventral retina—for seeing above—sees better in blue to discriminate predatory birds against a blue sky, while the dorsal retina—for seeing below—sees better in green to discriminate predatory land mammals against green foliage."

Speaking of colors, rabbit irises, which surround the pupil, are wonderfully diverse in their pigmentation: bright blue, dark brown, light brown, and grayish-blue are all common, and they tend to darken with age. Some rabbits, such as New Zealand Whites, have no eye pigmentation; ocular blood vessels make their transparent irises appear pink. Incidentally, rabbits have a nictitating membrane, a transparent "third eyelid" that covers the eyes when they are sleeping, giving the impression that they are awake.

What you may notice upon spotting a rabbit in nature is how much they rely on their large outer ears, or pinnas, which they can rotate 270 degrees to detect the source of sounds. Even more remarkably, each pinna can swivel independently, allowing them to monitor two separate sounds at the same time. Rabbits have excellent hearing, though the data on just how good differs depending on the source. Some researchers estimate the rabbit's frequency range to be 96–49,000 Hertz, or vibrations per second, while others put it at 360–42,000 Hertz. Either way, their hearing is about twice as good as that of humans, which comes in at a mere 64–23,000 Hertz. Still, rabbits are not the organisms with the greatest audible range. In fact, they're not even in the top ten, which currently consists of bats, cats, dogs, dolphins, elephants, horses, owls, rats, pigeons, and moths, the latter of whom are regarded as having the best hearing of anyone (up to 300,000 Hertz—superhero hearing) and can even perceive the ultrasonic probes of bats who are looking to eat them.

With ears that curve inward like a slender funnel, rabbits can lie hidden in tall grass and still perceive sounds around them, including high-pitched sounds from birds, insects, rodents, and bats from very far away. There is even anecdotal evidence to suggest that rabbits eavesdrop on the conversations of songbirds and squirrels, who chatter when they feel it's safe to vocalize and thus offer cues that there is no danger nearby.

The rabbit's ears also play an important role in body language, and we can often discern what they are communicating by observing how they rotate or place them. When a bunny's ears are flat back, it usually means they are comfortable and content. It can also indicate they are asking to be groomed, especially if they lower their head. This posture can be confusing, though, because ears in the flat-back position can sometimes mean the rabbit is frightened. (Another rabbit would probably know for sure of course, but we can only guess.) With their ears upright and rotated forward, a rabbit is alert, cautiously scanning for any hint of danger. If the rabbit is ready to relax but still a bit wary, they might have one ear up and the other down. In a playful mood, rabbits often shake their ears; this is frequently a precursor to the rabbit jumping in the air and twisting their body — what bunny lovers have come to call a "binky," a spirited display that is a clear sign the rabbit is happy.

Along with long ears, rabbits are known for their noses, which seem to be perpetually twitching, even when they are relaxing. In addition to inhaling oxygen, the rabbit's nose is taking in information, sniffing the air for traces of scent, which are clues to their environment. Rabbits have 100 million olfactory receptors, or scent cells, giving them a highly developed sensory organ. (By comparison, a dog's nose has between 200 million to one billion, depending on the breed, and a human just six million.) Because a rabbit uses their sniffer to explore the world, you'll notice how quickly it wiggles when they come near something especially interesting — the faster the nose twitches, the more of its receptors are exposed. A rabbit investigating a human friend, for instance, might wiggle their nose 120 times a minute and then later slow the tempo to 20 times a minute. They might use their nose to give you a little bump, which may be interpreted as a request for attention or a gentle warning that you're in the way. Working together with the nose is the rabbit's upper lip, called a philtrum, which is divided and spreads a bit as the nose does its thing, moistening the molecules it draws in and making the scent they carry even more distinct. They also use their lips to bring food into their mouth.

Surrounding the rabbit's nose — and indeed most of the face — is an intricate set of whiskers, some of which extend to the entire width of the body. Because these whiskers vibrate when touched and are attached to sensory nerves at the base, they help rabbits navigate in the dark as well as measure the width of holes and passageways so they know whether or not they will fit. It's pretty ingenious, actually. In fact, humans used to have whiskers, too. Somehow, around 800,000 years ago, our DNA evolved to eliminate them. Perhaps these early *Homo sapiens* figured out that lying was a more practical way to get out of tight spots and not have to walk around looking like Salvador Dali or Captain Hook.

A Very Long Life

Although rabbits can live about ten years in the safety of someone's home, a rabbit named Flopsy lived to a truly grand old age, at least according to *The Guinness Book of World Records*. Caught in the wild on August 6, 1964, Flopsy reportedly died 18 years, 10 months, and 21 days later at the home of L. B. Walker in Longford, Tasmania, Australia.

Anyone who has ever offered a rabbit a piece of strawberry or banana knows that they are fond of sweet foods. But what else do we know about the rabbit's sense of taste? Not a whole lot, it turns out. The common wisdom is that rabbits have about 17,000 taste buds, compared to our 10,000 or so, and can distinguish between sweet, sour, salty, and bitter. Little wonder, then, that house rabbits enjoy a variety of vegetables, herbs, fruits (in moderation), and even different hays. That rabbit you are fortunate enough to observe in the wild or in your garden is likely eating—or looking for food—and they are using their fine-tuned taste buds to tell the healthy plants from the toxic ones.

Chewing those delicious foods are 28 teeth that are "unrooted," meaning the root does not close at the base of the tooth but stays open so they can continue to grow. That's right, the rabbit's teeth never stop growing—about one-eighth of an inch (2–3 mm) a week, on average. This is nature's way of ensuring that all the abrasive plants in the bunny's diet don't eventually wear the two upper incisors, two lower incisors, six upper premolars, four lower premolars, six upper molars, six lower molars, and two peg-like auxiliary incisors behind the upper incisors down to the gums. (It is in part because of these extra incisors that since 1912 rabbits have no longer been classified as rodents, who only have one set, but as lagomorphs, though many people still refer to them as rodents.) It's also an essential reason house rabbits need to eat plenty of fibrous hay every day. Their teeth are arranged so that they are sharpened by wear against the opposing teeth, creating fine-edged instruments that can easily slice through tough veggies, grind coarse twigs, or snip through your phone cord when you're on an important call. The teeth of companion rabbits should be regularly checked to guard against them becoming overgrown, at which point they will need to be trimmed by a veterinarian. (Rabbit guardians will find a qualified vet to be the best source of advice for their bunny's well-being.)

As the food travels from the mouth through the twists and turns of the rabbit's gastrointestinal tract, it will eventually make it past the colon as one of two types of droppings. The first, commonly known as fecal pellets, are round and dry and mostly comprised of undigested fiber. These are what house rabbits leave in the litter box and what nature lovers might see on a forest floor. The second type are called caecals (or sometimes cecotropes or caecotrophs) and are not really feces but nutrient-packed dietary supplements—kind of like energy bars for bunnies (and hares, who also produce them).

Because they eat primarily high-fiber plants such as grass and hay, rabbits must consume a large quantity to meet their nutrient requirements. But their gastrointestinal tract is small, and the forage moves through quickly. To make the most of what they eat, rabbits repeat the digestion process by producing and then consuming caecals. These soft pellets, which resemble a tiny cluster of brown grapes covered in a membrane of mucus, are formed in the caecum. If you imagine the intestines as a winding road, the caecum is a cul-de-sac in the rabbit's lower abdomen where some food material pulls over to the curb. Bacteria and fungal organisms in the caecum create a fermentation chamber, converting food components into the vitamins, amino acids, and fatty acids essential to rabbit health. Caecals are generally eaten straight from the oven, so to speak, so you usually won't find evidence of them. If you've seen a rabbit who looks like they're cleaning their belly and then comes up chewing, you've no doubt witnessed a rabbit eating caecals—one of their favorite snacks. After being reingested, the caecals will be broken down, their nutrients and water extracted, and eventually become part of the fiber excreted as dry pellets. (By the way, humans have a caecum, too, though its function is merely to absorb salts and fluids after digestion, thank goodness.)

Whatever the activity—observing the environment, sleeping, or even eating and digesting food—everything a rabbit does is of course controlled by their brain. One of the most remarkable characteristics of the rabbit brain is that it lacks gyrification, a fancy word for the convolutions or intricate folds that often cover the outer layer of a brain's cerebral cortex. Such gyrification is abundant in human brains and in the brains of other predatory animals, and it supposedly indicates a higher order of mental processing, but the rabbit's brain is completely smooth. This is not to say that rabbits aren't intelligent, only that they are not required to function in the same ways that other animals are. Clearly, rabbits do a terrific job replicating their numbers, and they have all the intelligence they need to forage for food, build burrows, and adapt to diverse environments. Rabbits living indoors with humans are smart enough to learn a different set of skills, such as recognizing their names and other words and learning how to use a litter box, for example.

In 2018, researchers based in Sweden, Spain, and Portugal used magnetic resonance imaging (a high-resolution MRI) to view the brains of both wild and tame rabbits raised under similar conditions to better understand why the two behave so differently. Rabbits in nature are extremely skittish, with a remarkable flight response, while domesticated rabbits tend to be docile and quite at ease with humans. The scientists discovered three profound differences. First, wild rabbits have a larger brain-to-body size ratio than domesticated rabbits. Second, domesticated rabbits have a smaller amygdala, the area that detects physical threats, and an enlarged medial prefrontal cortex, which controls such decision-making as how one responds to perceived threats. And third, they found that domesticated rabbits have a reduction in white matter—the nerve fibers responsible for connecting regions of the brain into functioning circuits—suggesting that they are less able to process information, and that could help explain why they are more unflappable than their feral brethren.

All this makes perfect sense. Wild rabbits are constantly on guard, on the lookout for hawks, coyotes, and other predators. Most domesticated rabbits—particularly companion rabbits— enjoy an infinitely easier existence, not even having to concern themselves with locating food. The researchers expected to find differences in the brains, but the magnitude of those differences was a revelation. The amygdala of a domesticated rabbit, for instance, was typically 10 percent smaller. The full implications of these brain changes are not entirely clear, though many rabbit experts advise guardians of domesticated rabbits that their companion's intelligence means that they can get bored, so they need activities and other diversions to stay happy. They respond to affection and attention and delight in being talked to.

As we've seen, rabbits have a keen sense of smell, and this sense supports another type of communication in which they quickly rub their chins on surfaces. This is called "chinning," and it's a form of territorial behavior—a way for the rabbit to say "This is mine" or "I've been here" or "I can't drive, but I like the look of these car keys." Within the rabbit's chin are submandibular glands that secrete a scent on the skin surface. The scent is undetectable by the paltry noses of humans, but for rabbits it is an important part of marking what they like, whether it's a water bowl, a toy, or another rabbit. Likewise, companion rabbits often chin objects they would seem to have little use for, such as a coat rack, garden rock, or TV remote control. Chinning these things is mainly a preemptive measure intended to dissuade a new rabbit who might come into the house from thinking they have any right to use, say, your stereo speakers or ironing board.

For mating purposes, the chinned scent also helps female rabbits discriminate between dominant and subordinate males, and that transitions us neatly into a brief look at rabbit reproduction. Rabbits are prolific procreators, which is one way nature helps their populations flourish. Reaching sexual maturity at anywhere from three to eight months of age, a female rabbit will theoretically be fertile for another decade or so (rabbits in the home live much longer than rabbits in the wild), and in her lifetime she can potentially have a remarkably large number of babies, called kittens or kits. (By one estimate, a pair of house rabbits could hypothetically result in a breathtaking 3,745,584 offspring in four years.) In the wild, cottontail rabbits often engage in a ritual biologists call "cavorting," with the male and female running, chasing, hopping and twisting high into the air, and even fighting. As a result, it's not uncommon to find fragments of fur strewn over several acres. All these acrobatics are evidently part of cottontail courtship, intended to help the female determine if a potential mate is healthy and aggressive enough to dip into her gene pool.

Because they are "induced ovulators," female rabbits can

become pregnant at practically any moment; rather than being "in heat" during certain times, courtship and the sex act itself stimulate ovulation. Once pregnant, she will gestate for about 30 days before giving birth to between four and 12 kits. She can get pregnant again the same day, which is one reason it is so important to have house rabbits spayed and neutered. The newborns themselves are hairless, their eyes are closed, and they are completely dependent on their mothers. They are also about the cutest infants you've ever seen, with tiny ears and feet that only hint at the beautiful animals they will grow into. With most wild rabbits, all this magic happens underground, where the mother will have excavated a nesting chamber about the size of a cantaloupe near her burrow (maybe with help from the father, though more likely not). The mother lines the subterranean chamber with grass and her own fur and conceals the entrance with vegetation. Here she will nurse and care for her little ones until they are about three weeks old. Eastern cottontail rabbits, who are common in the United States, are an exception, as they often build shallow aboveground nests for their babies, rather than in an underground chamber. Both in the wild and in the home, mother rabbits spend time away from their offspring, though usually not far off, returning at dawn or dusk to feed them. This is partly because the adult rabbit knows that she has a scent while her babies do not, and therefore she could attract the attention of a predator.

A mother's scent is critical to the survival of the newborn kits, who are functionally deaf and blind at birth, as their ears are folded back and their eyes are sealed shut for about the first 10 to 12 days. In the meantime, they rely on their sense of smell to detect their mother. Even in the womb, rabbits can smell the protective amniotic fluid that surrounds them, and once born they are able to pick out this odor in their mother, which leads them to a lactating nipple for nursing. Further aiding the kit in their sightless search for nourishment is a mammary pheromone the mother releases and the kit smells — a way for nature to say, "Follow your nose, hungry baby, to a source of milk." After several days, the kits begin actively nibbling on and eventually consuming some of the hard fecal pellets their mother has deposited in the nest. Scientists believe this practice may help the young rabbits later identify adult members of their colony and may promote the rapid transfer of important gut microflora to the kit's digestive system. Kits also gradually begin eating nest material in the form of grass and other vegetation that has traces of their mother's scent before adopting an adult diet.

About a week after birth, the babies start to grow fur, which is the rabbit's most characteristic feature, especially the color and pattern. Though some rabbits and hares living in nature are white, most are brown or grayish-brown. This appearance, called the "agouti pattern," is actually the result of a yellow band in the middle of an otherwise dark hair shaft and is quite common among mammals. A rabbit's fur may darken or lighten as they age, but snowshoe hares are unique in the lagomorph world since they can change color to help them blend in with their surroundings: they are white in the snowy winter and then reddish-brown in the spring and summer. Such background matching helps lagomorphs in other environments, as well; rabbits and hares tend to be paler in the desert, darker in forests and woodlands, and more reddish and gray in rocky habitats.

Domesticated rabbits, who have been bred for color as well as size and shape, can have brown fur, gray fur, white fur, black fur, or some combination of colors. Members of the breed known as Harlequin, for instance, have fur that is either mostly orange or mostly white with a pattern of black, blue, brown, or lavender. Dutch rabbits, meanwhile, are easily identified by their pattern of color, which is either black, gray, dark brown, light brown, or blue. The color appears on their lower body, looking like well-tailored pants, and on their ears and face like a Mardi Gras eye mask, leaving their upper body, feet, and middle of their face white. The short fur of Rex rabbits is exceptionally soft and dense, with the feel of plush velvet. Their fur might be black, white, amber, blue, lavender, patterned with spots, or in a shade of brown. Angora rabbits have long fur that is silky and delicate. Whatever the color or pattern, a rabbit's fur insulates their body, keeps them warm, and helps prevent sunburn.

In Defense of White Rabbits

People who adopt rabbits tend to favor those with colorful fur or markings, overlooking many all-white rabbits. This is a shame, because white rabbits— specifically the New Zealand White and the American White—are loaded with personality. While other bunnies can be shy or feisty, these rabbits are generally very confident, playful, and calm, at least all those I have had the pleasure to know. Some people aren't fond of the white rabbit's pink eyes, but they are actually quite beautiful and resemble rubies. Give a white rabbit your love and affection and you will have made a true friend.

Rabbits are exceptionally clean, and they groom themselves by licking their fur (they clean their ears by first licking their front paws and gliding them over their ears). In rabbit colonies, whether in the wild or in your home, grooming is an important part of social interaction and hierarchy, with higher-ranking bunnies being groomed by subordinate ones. The dominant rabbit will demand a grooming by putting their head down low, placing it near the chin of the other rabbit.

Some rabbits develop an extra layer of fur-covered flesh around their neck, just below the jaw. Known as a dewlap, this layer can be remarkably pronounced in females, especially those who are pregnant and in certain breeds, such as New Zealand Whites, Lops, and Flemish Giants. Because mother rabbits pull out tufts of their own fur to line nests, the dewlap provides an extra source from which to pluck. Older rabbits may use their dewlap for warmth, lying with their faces pressed into it.

Unlike cats, rabbits don't cough up hairballs—nor, indeed, do they regurgitate at all—so rabbit guardians need to watch for signs that their rabbit may be suffering from a buildup of fur in their gut. Such a buildup can lead to an intestinal blockage and a serious condition known as gastrointestinal stasis, sometimes called GI stasis or simply stasis. This is a common disorder in which rabbits become listless, do not eat, and leave very small or no fecal droppings. A bunny in GI stasis usually requires an immediate visit to a rabbit-savvy veterinarian. Frequent brushing of a companion rabbit is one way to minimize stasis, though there can be other causes besides fur.

The skeleton represents just 7 to 8 percent of the rabbit's body weight—about half the percentage of a human's—making them rather delicate animals. Portions of their skull have lattice-like holes called fenestration to help reduce the weight. Like humans, rabbits are susceptible to arthritis and osteoporosis as they age. If rabbits are not held securely when picked up, their kicking can actually result in a vertebral fracture.

What they lack in bone mass they make up for in muscle, however, which comprises half of their body weight and gives them powerful limbs for propulsion, whether they are sprinting across a field or displaying that most characteristic of all rabbit moves: the hop. Technically, rabbits are not really hoppers; that is, they do not depend on hopping to get from point A to point B—at least not like true hoppers such as kangaroos and wallabies, who rely solely on their hindlimbs for swift locomotion. Instead, they have what biologist Rachel Simons describes as a "half-bound gait," in which their hindlimbs work in tandem but their forelimbs land separately. Dr. Simons, who specializes in the biomechanics of movement, says rabbits may hop when they are moving very slowly, as when they graze.

"But as soon as they start to travel at any reasonable speed, they use the half-bound: hindlimbs together, forelimbs landing sequentially. And when they speed up, they retain this same gait pattern. So, their gait remains the same, even as speed increases."

However we may define hopping, I think anyone who's witnessed a rabbit go from a sedate, seated position to suddenly springing vertically into the air like a pole-vaulter would be hard-pressed to call the feat anything but a bona fide hop. Such an achievement calls for immensely powerful hindlegs, and these also come in handy for thumping. When a rabbit senses danger, they may raise their back feet and thump the ground. It's one of the most evident signs of rabbit communication and is used to warn other rabbits in the colony or express anger or concern. "The rest of the rabbit's body remains very tense and alert during this motion, although the rabbit often moves his head from side to side as if looking for what's startling him," write Susan Davis and Margo DeMello in *Stories Rabbits Tell*.

A rabbit might also use their hindlegs to direct displeasure toward someone in particular. If you live with a house rabbit, you might notice them spring away from you and add a little flick to their back feet, like they're shaking imaginary dust off their heels. They might do this after you've clipped their nails, shooed them away from chewing on the legs of your antique desk, or in the wake of some other perceived injustice. It's often their way of saying they are peeved at you, though you'll generally find that they have forgotten all about it in a moment or two.

The rabbit's feet have been considered lucky by some cultures, but certainly no one needs a rabbit's foot more than rabbits themselves. With hard nails, for instance, the feet are especially adept at digging tunnels and burrows. (Because house rabbits don't use their nails except to satisfy an occasional itch and thus don't wear them down, they rely on their human friends to give them periodic pedicures.) Underneath the feet are no footpads, like some species; instead, thick fur covering part of the foot provides shock absorption between their skin and the ground. The lack of footpads is one of the many reasons rabbits should never be kept in a cage.

Finally, as the rabbit you've been spying in your garden or in nature scurries away, your eyes are drawn to their tail, that white ball of fluff that has puzzled scientists for centuries. Why is it, they wonder, that a prey animal would have brown fur to camouflage themselves yet also have such a flashy protuberance on their rump? Is it used as a warning sign to other bunnies? Does it figure in attracting mates? You'd think the last thing an animal trying to disguise themselves would have is the equivalent of a neon light on their backside. But it turns out that's the genius of rabbit biology, at least according to evolutionary biologist Dirk Semmann, who in 2013 announced that he'd solved the mystery of the rabbit tail. He believes that the white tufts give rabbits in the wild the ability to outmaneuver predators. When chased, he explains, the rabbit makes quick, sharp turns, and whoever is pursuing them focuses on their bright appendage. (Rachel Simons estimates that a motivated cottontail can sprint at 30 miles an hour, or 48 km/h.) With the rabbit darting here and then there, the tail momentarily disappears, disorienting the predator and forcing them to refocus.

"I came up with the idea during my PhD thesis while I was running," explains Dr. Semmann, who is now a professor at the University of Göttingen in Germany. He would often meet a particular rabbit on the trail, and he started wondering why a prey animal would have such a conspicuous marking. "On first sight, the rabbit seemed easier to follow than without the mark. That seemed to me like an evolutionary disadvantage, and as an evolutionary biologist I knew that traits disappear over time if they are not to the individual's advantage." As the rabbit would run, Dr. Semmann could easily follow their movement, especially with the white tail to guide his eyes. "Then suddenly the rabbit would turn off the trail in an almost ninety-degree turn," he says. "For me it was very difficult to tell whether they had turned left or right. At this point I noticed that I had only concentrated on the flashing of the white tail, and suddenly this signal was turned off due to the change in the body axis of the rabbit." These continual rapid turns, he says, add up to valuable seconds that help rabbits escape.

As the dawn calls forth illumination or dusk inevitably surrenders to darkness, our friend the wild rabbit will return to the safety of their burrow. Did they see you standing there, quietly observing them? Did they sense you with their powerful ears or perhaps smell your scent? If they did so without scampering off, you are truly privileged indeed. But if they fled before you could admire them from afar, do not be disheartened. A rabbit sighting may be rare in some places, but you can always adopt a rabbit from a shelter or rescue group, if you haven't already. The idea of living with a bunny is hardly new, but as more people come to know these animals, and more veterinarians are learning to treat them, they are becoming less "exotic" and more everyday. They make wonderful companions.

Chapter Nine

Rabbits in the Home

House rabbits are not a fad. They are not Easter toys. They are year-round companions to millions of people around the world.

—Marinell Harriman, *House Rabbit Handbook*

Ask nearly anyone who keeps a rabbit in a backyard hutch without giving them any freedom, and they couldn't begin to tell you about that bunny's personality. To them, I'll wager, the rabbit mostly just sits quietly, observing the world through a wire door. The only interaction they might have with the bunny is when they check their water bottle or feed them. Little or no consideration is given to weather conditions or predators, who can still frighten someone in a cage. This a very sad state for any animal, especially one with so much capacity for joy—an animal who craves companionship, autonomy, and the ability to give full rein to their longing for exercise. Passing their days and nights in a hutch is no way for them to live. Fortunately, there's a growing movement that embraces the house rabbit.

As popular practices go, living with a rabbit or two (or more) indoors—where they have the freedom and safety to explore and hop and groom and binky and nap and essentially just be themselves—is actually a fairly recent development, at least in humanity's history with companion animals, which is also not that old. In her book *Pets in America: A History*, Katherine Grier observes that keeping domesticated animals for companionship became widespread in the nineteenth century, when it was strongly associated with childhood. "For both children and adults, caring for pets was one avenue for the cultivation of the self through expressive behavior during moments of leisure," she writes. "At its best, the practice fostered gentle emotions, curiosity about the world, and even aesthetic appreciation."

Keeping rabbits as pets was especially encouraged for boys, who were thought to be more prone to immoral behavior and would thus have something wholesome to occupy their idle hours. It also supposedly prepared a boy for his future role as the head of a household, in which he would provide shelter, food, and protection for his wife and children. For Victorian girls, rabbits were often considered surrogate babies who allegedly needed the attention only a make-believe mother could provide. But some commentators cautioned against giving rabbits too much affection, perhaps fearing children would elevate their cherished bunny to the status of an actual human. A character in Mary Claude's 1854 book *Natural History in Stories for Little Children*, for instance, warns her nephew that carrying his rabbit into the house could be dangerous for the bunny and tells him of a rabbit who was once brought inside and accidentally came to grief on a knitting needle.

In the early 1800s, the breeding of "fancy" rabbits became a pastime in England. A rabbit with two or more colors was considered "fancy," but this appellation was bestowed upon lop-eared bunnies beginning with the first English Lop, recorded in 1822. Fancy rabbit clubs met regularly to admire bunnies and award prizes to competitors (all men) based on such criteria as rabbits with the longest ears, heaviest weight, and "best" colors. With every member entering several rabbits for competition, another highlight was for judges to measure the length of each bunny and determine which group had the largest sum total in inches. These gatherings were also opportunities for members to congratulate themselves on, in their view, improving upon nature. Reporting on a meeting in 1848, a writer for the British weekly newspaper *The Era* noted: "Many magnificent specimens of this particular breed of domesticated animals, evincing in a surprising degree the improvement effected by the care of man, were exhibited, and the company, after the usual complimentary toasts to the chairman, judges, and office-bearers, separated well-pleased with the evening's reunion." I believe the writer meant "species" rather than "breed," but whatever.

With so much interest in rabbit colors, sizes, and shapes, breeders set to work selectively mating pairs with unique characteristics so that we now have Flemish Giants sitting beside Netherland Dwarfs, New Zealand Whites befriending Baladi Blacks, Harlequins dancing with Himalayans, French Angoras grooming English Spots and Holland Lops, and many more. The Belgian Hare, so popular with Beatrix Potter and her contemporaries, was the result of breeding wild rabbits with their domesticated cousins in Flanders; they were brought to England in the 1870s and then to the United States in 1888. All of these rabbits are descendants of common ancestors who were isolated on the Iberian Peninsula and small parts of France and northwest Africa during the last Ice Age roughly 18,000 years ago.

By the 1940s, media stories about Easter were offering advice not only on how to care for rabbits but how to treat them as members of the household. "So, there may be pleasure in contemplation of the fact that rabbits can be house broken to a box, like a cat," wrote one columnist. "Yes, they can! It's been done, right here in Washington. ... Of course, the training took time, but from reports seemed well worth it." The writer's encouraging tone almost makes up for her suggesting that one suitable treat for rabbits is chocolate, which we now know can be toxic to them.

It was sometime in the latter part of the last century that rabbits truly transcended the "pet" description to become "family" on a large scale, living indoors with people and leading lives that are deeply entangled—emotionally and physically—with others in the home. The movement got a boost in the 1980s, after Marinell Harriman and her husband, Bob, noticed a large, white-and-black rabbit in their backyard in Alameda, California. They scooped her up and brought her inside, where the Harriman children promptly fell in love with her. The family named her Herman. Bob had grand plans to build her an outdoor hutch, but as the weeks passed and Herman remained inside, she charmed everyone, including the dog and cat. She learned her name and figured out how to open the door of Marinell and Bob's bedroom, where she insisted on sleeping with them. "Herman entranced our whole household," Marinell says. "So finally we said to each other, 'Herman has obviously become a member of the family. Can we force her to go live in the yard?'"

The Harrimans knew nothing about domesticated rabbits and found no books on the subject anywhere, so Marinell resorted to posting notices on the bulletin boards of local pet stores, asking if anyone else was living with a bunny. After connecting with a number of fellow rabbit enthusiasts, she began collecting their stories. She also learned a lot from Herman, who inspired her to become a vegetarian. In 1985, Marinell coined the term "house rabbit" with the publication of her groundbreaking book *House Rabbit Handbook: How to Live with an Urban Rabbit*, which explains how to keep rabbits healthy and happy in a human environment. A year later, she and Bob rescued four more rabbits from an animal shelter in nearby Oakland, brought them home, and placed ads in local newspapers to find suitable adopters. Within no time the shelter was calling them directly, and Bob and Marinell found themselves fostering rabbits, training them to use a litter box, and finding loving homes for them. Marinell, Bob, and several of their colleagues soon saw the need for a nonprofit organization that would advocate for and help rescue these animals, and so they founded the House Rabbit Society

(HRS) in January of 1988.

Such an advocacy group was badly needed. In the same year that HRS was launched, for example, a lengthy article in Missouri's *St. Joseph Gazette* advised readers to keep pet rabbits locked up in a small hutch and feed them only pellets—there is no mention of their need for fresh hay or veggies, let alone enrichment or companionship (indeed, it even declares that rabbits "are best kept solitary").

Beguiling Bunnies

Marinell Harriman will be the first to tell you that the world is fascinated by rabbits. "In the spring of 1988, the newly formed House Rabbit Society had decided to launch an educational newsletter on rabbit care," she says. "My husband, Bob, who had a background in magazine production, searched for a local printer with a small press who could handle our job. When we met the new printer and he found out that this was going to be an ongoing newsletter, he was puzzled. He asked, 'Aren't you going to run out of things to say— about rabbits?' That question has not been asked since then, as an ever-growing number of books, magazines, websites, blogs, lectures, and personal conversations answer it every day. We never run out of things to say about rabbits."

Of course, humans have been cohabitating with bunnies well before the 1980s. A century earlier, the English author and illustrator Beatrix Potter brought home a Belgian Hare she named Benjamin Bouncer, who lived in her London house at least part of the time and tolerated a collar and leash for walks. Benjamin would become the model for most of the rabbits she drew in the 1890s for greeting cards and other illustrations that predated her books such as *The Tale of Peter Rabbit* (1902) and *The Tale of Tom Kitten* (1907). And he was the inspiration for the title character in *The Tale of Benjamin Bunny* (1904). Benjamin was followed by Peter Piper, another Belgian Hare, who enjoyed relaxing on a rug by the fire. The two clearly had distinct personalities. Ms. Potter described Peter as "an affectionate companion and quiet friend," while Benjamin was "inclined to attack strangers." Revealing the comical side of life with rabbits that so many bunny guardians can identify with today, she wrote in 1892: "Benjamin once fell into an Aquarium head first and sat in the water which he could not get out of, pretending to eat a piece of string. Nothing like putting a face upon circumstances."

We can go back even further to find examples of early adopters. William Cowper, an eighteenth-century English poet, was a rabbit enthusiast who is perhaps best known today for his anti-slavery and nature poetry. Mr. Cowper (pronounced "Cooper") influenced the literature of his day by writing of common, everyday life, and for him, nothing was more common than sharing his house with companion animals. His cousin Harriett Hesketh noted that "he had at one time five rabbits, three hares, two guinea pigs, a magpie, a jay, and a starling; besides two goldfinches, two canary birds, and two dogs. It is amazing how the three hares can find room to gambol and frolic (as they certainly do) in his small parlour."

Of all the animals who occupied William Cowper's home in Olney, Buckinghamshire, it is the hares—actual hares, not the Belgian variety—that we know the most, since he left behind much writing about them. In 1774, he accepted a young hare as a gift from some neighborhood children, and then shortly two more from his neighbors, who were only too pleased to make the rather solemn poet happy. He named them Bess, Puss, and Tiney, and he grew close to each one. Puss (a common name at the time for hares and rabbits as well as cats) was the friendliest, and he enjoyed being carried about in Mr. Cowper's arms and even falling asleep on his knee. Tiney was a bit grumpy, preferring to play on his own. Bess was remarkably confident and fearless. The poet writes that "One evening the cat, being in the room, had the hardiness to pat Bess upon the cheek, an indignity which he resented by drumming upon her back with such violence that the cat was happy to escape from under his paws, and hide herself." (How it was that Lady Hesketh had managed to overlook the cat's presence in the house history does not tell us.)

He may have been irritable, but when Tiney died in 1783 at eight years and five months of age, William Cowper penned a moving tribute to his friend, "Epitaph on a Hare," one of his most celebrated poems. Filled with beautiful imagery, the elegy captures Tiney's big personality, as in this stanza:

> *A Turkey carpet was his lawn,*
> *Whereon he loved to bound,*
> *To skip and gambol like a fawn,*
> *And swing his rump around.*

And, um, this one:

> *Though duly from my hand he took*
> *His pittance every night,*
> *He did it with a jealous look,*
> *And, when he could, would bite.*

Thus it is with genuine affection and humor that Mr. Cowper immortalized Tiney. (And it is clear that his love of animals and belief in their sentience is one reason he condemned blood sports, as he did in his 1785 poem "The Task.") Incidentally, Cowper's contemporary and fellow abolitionist William Wilberforce also had pet hares at home. In addition to being a leading voice in England's anti-slavery movement, he would go on to cofound the Royal Society for the Prevention of Cruelty to Animals in 1824.

Royal Rabbit

Designed by architect Christopher Wren in 1709, Marlborough House in London has been home to many illustrious citizens. One such resident was Alexandra of Denmark (1844–1925), known in the mid nineteenth century as the Princess of Wales, who would become queen to King Edward VII in 1902 and was widely known for her love of animals. In the garden of the mansion is a small pet cemetery, and among the tiny gravestones is one that reads: "Bonny, Favourite Rabbit of H.R.H. the Princess of Wales, Died June 8, 1881."

Although I would never recommend taking an animal from the wild and bringing them home, as Cowper and Wilberforce demonstrate, hares have occasionally become companions to humans. In 1953, Cecil Webb, superintendent of the Dublin Zoo, and his wife, also a member of the zoo staff, were handed a day-old Irish Hare in the hope that they could help the little leveret survive. The couple was accustomed to hand-rearing abandoned animals, so they weren't surprised when their furry dependent flourished. What they didn't expect was that his affection and personality would so completely enchant them that he'd become a permanent part of their family with full access to the house. They named him Horace and were delighted with his fastidious cleaning habits and how quickly he learned to use a litter box, or in this case a cooking pot lined with sand (litter boxes and trays were just catching on in the 1950s). They were equally pleased when he became friends with Squirt, a newborn white rabbit the Webbs rescued two weeks later. Still a baby himself, Horace took on the role of the little rabbit's guardian, "washing him from head to foot and apparently worried if Squirt was not looking as immaculate as himself," wrote Cecil in his 1955 book *A Hare About the House*. "The attachment grew and grew and they became inseparable companions to a degree rarely seen in animals of any kind."

The two may have been the best of friends, but they certainly had their differences. While Squirt was something of a grouch, for instance, Horace loved nothing more than when Cecil played with him. "To get him really excited it is best to chase him clapping one's hands, and then he tears off leaping and twisting in the air and zig-zagging at great speed." And as a wild animal at heart, Horace proved adept at escaping the house several times and sprinting away on some outdoor adventure, though he could always be coaxed back inside. "In contrast to this Squirt was quite placid—content to sit on any rug in front of a fire with no desire to know what was at the back of beyond or even in the next room."

Abraham Lincoln also had a soft spot for rabbits. In 1862, shortly after the president and Mrs. Lincoln lost their son Willie to typhoid fever, a Philadelphia man named Michael Crock had a pair of white bunnies delivered to the White House as a gift to help console their grieving eight-year-old son, Tad. Although the rabbits were housed in the stables, along with pet goats and a turkey, by all accounts they were well loved. The president sent Crock a thank-you letter, noting that Tad was very pleased with them. President Lincoln rarely signed letters with his full name, but he did so in this case, perhaps as a way of expressing his deep gratitude.

Just how many rabbits live with humans today is a bit difficult to determine. As mentioned in Chapter One, many rabbit advocacy groups in the United States claim bunnies are the third most common companion animal in the country, but exact figures for rabbits are hard to come by. Based on surveys by the nonprofit American Pet Products Association (APPA), the House Rabbit Society calculated that there were about three million rabbits kept as pets in the USA in 2020, ranking them well below dogs and cats in popularity. To be fair, however, the number of pet fishes far surpasses dogs, cats, and rabbits—about 140 million fishes kept in freshwater aquariums, according to one estimate—though sadly people tend to regard these animals as a hobby or decoration rather than as companions.

According to a 2019–20 survey by the APPA, while the majority of small companion animals such as hamsters and guinea pigs live in households with children, the opposite is true for rabbits, most of whom live in homes *without* kids. Rabbit guardians are also more likely to say that these companions help relieve stress, are like family members, and are good for the family's health.

Whatever their place in the household polls, rabbits are undeniably popular. You might not conclude this from a visit to your local bookstore or library, however, where you'll discover the shelves positively brimming with colorful and engaging books on cats, dogs, and horses but nary a title on rabbits. If you find one at all it will likely be devoted to rabbit breeding, not the joy of having them as companions. (As I was doing research for this chapter, I asked my house rabbit contacts to recommend nonfiction books that feature an adopted bunny, and no one could offer a single suggestion.) Not only are books on rabbits as companions woefully underrepresented in the "pets" genre, but the narratives that are available vary widely, from presenting inept people who appear to have no business taking in a rabbit to those who rescue and truly cherish these animals as individuals.

Enslaved by Ducks rests securely in the former category and is the cautionary tale of a couple venturing into the world of rabbit guardianship without even the vaguest whisper of leporine knowledge between them. Early in the book by Bob

Tarte, he and his wife, Linda, buy an eight-week-old Dutch bun from a breeder (please do not buy animals from breeders), who assures them that they can phone him with any questions. The Tartes take the baby bunny home, name him Binky—after a rabbit in the *Life in Hell* comic strip by Matt Groening, not as an homage to any acrobatic dance moves—and proceed to ply him with buttered toast and tortilla chips in the misguided belief that rabbits thrive on a diet that's not even healthy for humans.

Predictably, the breeder knows nothing about rabbits beyond how they reproduce and how much money the average person is prepared to pay for one. When Linda calls him wondering why Binky chews on furniture or runs around their feet honking, he can only respond with, "I wish I had an answer for you" or "I've never run into that one before." An exasperated Bob finally admits, "We wondered how a person who made a profession of breeding rabbits could know so little about their behavior." The Tartes apparently make no effort to have Binky neutered, to bunny-proof their home, or to give him unlimited access to the fibrous hay needed to keep his teeth in check and his gut healthy. Instead, they spend most of their time trying to cajole Binky from within the impossibly small hiding places where he prefers to conceal himself. Perhaps Bob Tarte's wisest observation is, "When you match wits with a rabbit, you cannot win."

A much more inspiring book is Jeffrey Moussaieff Masson's *Raising the Peaceable Kingdom*, in which he explores the question of whether animals of five different species—a dog, a cat, two rats, a chicken, and a rabbit (a Flemish Giant) named Hohepa— could not only learn to live harmoniously if raised together in proximity but also form genuine friendships. The author and his family live in a beautiful beachfront home in Auckland, New Zealand, which I'm tempted to believe helped a lot. Although Masson had spent time with rabbits before, he admits that he doesn't know much about them, and he allows Hohepa outside during the day, trusting that he will return each night. He does, but he also digs his way into the neighbors' yards, sampling the greenery from their gardens and agitating their dogs, who have not agreed to participate in any sort of interspecies utopia. The neighbors complain, and Masson is obliged to keep Hohepa inside except for supervised time on the lawn. With an insatiable appetite for alfresco adventure, not to mention next-door botanicals, Hohepa seems miserable in the house and manages to escape several times, once disappearing for two days.

Eventually making Hohepa's time indoors more tolerable is his relationship with Tamaiti the cat. The two animals, predator and prey, become best friends. Masson includes a photo of the cat and rabbit lounging together, eyes closed, with Tamaiti's left paw slung over Hohepa's shoulders in a gesture of pure affection. "If we hesitated to say that Hohepa was in love," he writes, "we could say he was infatuated, for he would spend all his time waiting for Tamaiti and when he saw him would rush over to greet him. Groom him. Kiss him (or were they little love bites?). Dote on him." I admire the premise of this book, and Jeffrey Masson's thoughtful observations and writing, very much, though I wish he had prepared himself with more knowledge about rabbits and their needs.

Focusing almost entirely on lagomorphs is *Touched by a Rabbit*, a collection of essays by devoted bunny admirers. Among them is Lisa Ivers, who writes lovingly of Jasper, an unwanted Easter bunny she rescued in 1999. Jasper is welcome anywhere in the house, and when two women from a certain religious order come inside to share their beliefs over a cup of coffee, she decides to sit on the headrest behind one of them. Lisa writes, "I never imagined that a rabbit could maintain such an unblinking stare at the back of someone's head." When the author moves Jasper down to the floor, the bunny finds other ways to express her displeasure. "In an instant she was rifling through the open purse of our guest, tossing keys, Kleenex, and unmentionable feminine hygiene products to the wind. ...

When my guest tried to recover her purse, she got a sound slap on the hand by a rogue rabbit paw, followed by an angry stamp and disgusted sniff. Jasper then retreated with a look that can only be translated as 'my work here is done.'"

The stories in *Touched by a Rabbit* range from humorous to heartfelt, reflecting the many ways bunnies impact our lives. Joe Marcom, a retired paramedic who volunteers for the Houston-based rescue group Bunny Buddies, describes his affinity for special needs rabbits and how well they adapt once they're given proper care and room to be themselves. Gus, for example, had been adopted twice from a shelter and was returned both times because he had glaucoma, for which treatment in rabbits is seldom successful. Joe fosters Gus, fully expecting him to become a permanent resident. "However," he writes, "within a very short time he was adopted by someone who had previously had a blind rabbit and was happy to give him the necessary care. I receive periodic updates, and Gus is doing very well in his new home." And he saves the leg of Sugarplum, a Californian with a rare bone infection. Rejecting the recommended treatment of amputation, Joe treats Sugarplum's leg with antibiotics. Six months later, she was hopping around normally and soon found a forever home.

What makes the stories in this latter book "just right" is not only the focus on rabbits, but also the patience and love their guardians demonstrate to them. Every rabbit lover comes into this tableau with a unique set of knowledge and expectations. "Our bunnies continue to reveal their intricate personalities and social order and teach us to be more observant and efficient humans," writes Marinell Harriman in the fourth edition of *House Rabbit Handbook*.

The Cute Response
One reason for the prevalence of rabbits as a companion could be their appearance. Ethologist Konrad Lorenz

has suggested that such physical features as the rabbit's round face, large eyes, and small nose and mouth—traits we have come to call "cute"—elicit in us feelings of protectiveness and empathy, in large part because such characteristics are also found in human infants. These same features are commonly used in the creation of toy animals, such as Teddy bears, and cartoon characters, such as pretty much any protagonist produced by Disney.

My own initiation into the world of lagomorphs began shortly after I became an ethical vegan in 2001. I celebrated my new lifestyle by getting a tattoo of a rabbit, partly because I had an innate fondness for these gentle animals and partly because they are herbivorous. (Images of rabbits are also used on a growing number of products to indicate they haven't been tested on animals.) But I wanted to be a more active part of a movement advocating compassion for all, so I began volunteering at a local sanctuary for farmed animals, where they had a sizable colony of rabbits rescued from various unfortunate circumstances.

Bunny Health Check Day was my favorite time at the sanctuary. Once a month, several volunteers and a staff member would enter the large pen—a roofed area surrounded by chicken wire with a dirt floor—to give each rabbit a nail trim and inspect them for any signs of illness. The biggest challenge was gathering them into one small section first. You've no doubt heard the expression "like herding cats" used to describe some futile attempt at control. Well, trying to coax 25 energetic and skittish rabbits from their hiding places in burrows, hay bales, and cardboard tunnels was an exercise in patience and dexterity that would make most cat herders hang up their scratch-proof gloves.

The rabbits' lively personalities really became evident as we would try to corner one. Just as you were reaching down to carefully lift a rabbit into your arms, they would take off in an explosion of kinetic energy, leaving a cloud of dust in their wake and weaving through half a dozen pairs of pirouetting human legs until they'd found another hole in which to hide themselves. What I didn't understand at first is that most bunnies do not like to be picked up, though I learned this quickly, along with just how powerful a rabbit's kick can be—and what accurate aim they have. Needless to say, Bunny Health Check Day was not as much fun for them as it was for me.

Equipped with some rabbit experience, I contacted a local rescue nonprofit, SaveABunny (at the time a chapter of the House Rabbit Society), and asked about volunteering. The best way I could help, founder Marcy Berman told me, would be to foster a rabbit: bring a recently rescued bunny into my home and care for them until a permanent home could be found. I had never heard the term "foster failure" before, but I was about to become a true master of it.

Following Marcy's instructions, I "rabbit proofed" my apartment by placing electrical wires out of reach and moving valuable books onto higher shelves. A few days later, I had a large, neutered New Zealand White male as a roommate. Someone at SaveABunny had named him Buddy Boy, but I called him Nibbles. He was reserved and nervous if I approached him, so I respected his feelings and moved slowly and quietly when I was near him. But he was great about using his litter box, and he enjoyed the "hay bombs" I made for him—hay stuffed into a toilet paper tube.

A month or so later, I got a call from Marcy: SaveABunny had rescued a female New Zealand White who had been found beneath a car in San Francisco. Would I be willing to foster her, too, after she'd recovered from being spayed? I said yes; after all, I thought, two rabbits couldn't be much more work than one. "You'll have to keep her away from Nibbles," Marcy warned me, "or they might bond." Bonded bunnies are usually a good thing, she explained, but it can be harder to find a permanent home for two rabbits. I converted my dining area into a bunny room and welcomed a very dirty rabbit, her white fur still stained with motor oil. But I saw the elegant rabbit she was and named her Laxmi, after the Hindu goddess of beauty and well-being. She sprinted around the room with surprising confidence and was keenly curious about Nibbles.

Even with a wall of sturdy wooden boards between them, the two rabbits were clearly drawn to each other, and it seemed cruel to keep them apart. With Nibbles and Laxmi both sterilized, there was no danger of them reproducing. Besides, by this point I realized I had bonded with them, too; they were part of the family. The wall came down both literally and emotionally. I had failed at fostering, and I couldn't have been more pleased. It was so heartening to see how Laxmi adored Nibbles, and he returned her affection with tireless grooming. They were almost never apart, enjoying all their naps together and playfully chasing each other around the apartment. I built tunnels and cardboard houses for them and learned all I could about rabbit health and nutrition. The delight I felt in seeing them run and demonstrate their joy with binkies is indescribable.

I knew very little about their backgrounds before they came to live with me, but Marcy told me Nibbles had been terribly mistreated before being rescued. This made seeing him bond with Laxmi all the sweeter. I would have been content to let them be and just provide them a safe space to flourish, but they gradually accepted me as a friend. Laxmi was the first to take to me. She liked to jump on my stomach whenever I lay near them, and she relished being petted and talked to, softly grinding her teeth to express happiness. Nibbles was shy, but as he watched me interact with Laxmi, he seemed to understand I was a source of love and protection, and he too warmed up to me. Each morning, as I prepared a helping of pellets for their breakfast, he would run around my feet, quietly honking—another sign of rabbit happiness. How far you have come, I would think, amazed that any animal who had been abused could learn to trust a human. But rabbits have a remarkable power for forgiveness, and I saw this time and time again with other bunnies. Love and companionship appear to be second nature to them, and a wary bunny will usually embrace someone who treats them as a friend, even though this may take a while.

Nibbles and Laxmi spent most of their time together, but occasionally Laxmi would seek me out to see what I was up to. One afternoon I was sitting on the bedroom floor, my back against the bed, reading a chapter that described how cows and their calves are treated in the dairy industry. Laxmi was flopped on her side beneath the window, half asleep. It was an especially upsetting book, and I began to cry quietly. Laxmi suddenly lifted her head, looked at me, and sat up. As I wiped the tears off my face, she raised her back legs and thumped the carpeted floor loudly with her feet. She recognized something was amiss with me, and I can only imagine her thump—a gesture rabbits make when they sense danger or aren't sure what's going on— was meant to express her concern. I quickly scooted over to her and softly stroked her head, reassuring her everything was fine with me (though I was haunted by the dairy industry's practice of separating mother cows from their babies). It was then that I began to recognize the potential for the rabbit–human bond.

Among the first rabbits I had met during my initial visit to SaveABunny were Cameron and Peri, who were closely bonded. Cameron, tan and large, was infected with the parasite *E. cuniculi*, which is a common malady in rabbits. His mate Peri was a healthy black dwarf mix who was as feisty as he was gentle. Marcy had encouraged me to take these two as my first fosters, but I didn't feel I had enough experience to care for a "special needs" rabbit like Cameron, who required daily medication. As a result of the infection, Cameron's head was tilted, giving him a lopsided view of the world. Peri had stood by Cameron throughout his illness, and I loved her for that.

After a few months living with Nibbles and Laxmi, however, I decided to bring Cameron and Peri home and set them up in the spacious main bedroom. Even in his unsteady condition, Cameron was eager to explore his new surroundings, and he finally had room to run anytime he wished. Every day, I would use my thumb and forefinger to gingerly massage his neck, just above the shoulders, trying to ease the tense muscles. Weeks went by, and eventually I noticed something I never expected: Cameron's head was less tilted. Was it the exercise he was getting? The medication? The massages? A combination of all three? Whatever the reason, I was thrilled, and after a few months, his head was only the slightest bit askew. (Cameron was not cured of E. cuniculi, however, only one of the symptoms, so he would continue to receive medication throughout his life.) I could feel the renewed confidence in him as he played with Peri, keeping up with her leap for leap—or nearly so. And when I'd lie next to him, he would lick my forehead, grooming me. As any bunny person will tell you, that's the highest compliment a rabbit can bestow upon a human, and I was duly honored. I was now a four-time foster failure.

The next happy foster failure was a spunky gray rabbit named Frankie, who had a penchant for biting when you were at your most vulnerable, such as napping on the sofa or bending down to retrieve a pen from under the bed. One afternoon, as I lay on the carpet to stretch my back before a run, I glimpsed a smoky blur and then felt Frankie's incisors pierce the flesh of my left temple, narrowly missing my eyeball, which I use a lot. Despite his occasionally pugnacious behavior, he could be the most loving of rabbits and craved being held and talked to. Frankie, too, came to me with head tilt. Once again, a regimen of exercise, medication, and careful neck massages helped transform his condition. (I am not suggesting this technique will work for all rabbits with head tilt—also called wry neck—

but there's no question it did for Cameron and Frankie.)

Inevitably, rabbits passed away over the years, and I would assuage my grief by volunteering at the SaveABunny shelter in Mill Valley. It felt good to clean cages, groom rabbits, and help socialize the recently rescued ones for adoption. Once in a while, the shelter would care for a family of newborns and their mom. Holding one of these hairless babies, not yet even the size of my thumb, is always a powerful feeling. Like any baby, they each have a lifetime of experiences in their future, and I would always inaudibly wish for them the health and happiness they deserved.

At times I was reminded that some rabbits at the shelter need more careful attention than others, as when I prepared to clean the cage of a bunny named Alfonso. As I reached inside to pick him up, Alfonso bit my right hand so hard that his teeth left a permanent scar. "Oh, he's cage-protective," said Marcy, rushing for a bandage and a tube of antibiotic ointment. Indeed. On a few occasions I was overcome by a rabbit's sweetness, such as with Melville, a shy white-and-black Lop whose former guardian had not gotten him veterinary treatment after being attacked by a dog and so he had trouble using his back legs. I sensed Melville was not long for this world, and I didn't want him spending his final days in a shelter, so he became my first non-foster adoption.

Melville was a bachelor, and I believed having a rabbit friend would bring him more happiness, so I brought him back to SaveABunny for a bonding session—kind of like speed dating for bunnies. With his delicate spirit, Melville appeared to have difficulty connecting with anyone. But he eventually clicked with a beautiful, toffee-colored bunny with long lashes framing bottomless brown eyes. Those eyes and lashes inspired Marcy to name her Sophia Loren, after the Italian movie star. Sophia had been rescued by San Francisco Animal Control after being surrendered to a Bay Area shelter with 28 other rabbits. She and Melville had a tentative but friendly courtship, and upon believing theirs was a love match, I made my second non-foster adoption. After a few days, it was clear the name Sophie suited her better, so that's what I called her.

It was wonderful to see Melville enjoying Sophie's company, the two of them sleeping side by side and grooming each other. If they weren't as passionately devoted as Laxmi and Nibbles or Cameron and Peri, at least they had each other to share meals and discuss whatever issues or concerns house rabbits commiserate about (perhaps when the litter box would be cleaned or what the evening's veggie selection might be).

Being a Lop, Melville was especially prone to dental problems—they have been bred to look "cute," with an altered head shape that can affect the alignment of their teeth and jaw— and soon after I adopted him his veterinarian concluded that she would need to extract some of his back teeth. I scheduled an appointment for a Saturday two weeks later. "Since he's bonded with Sophie, bring her too," the vet advised. "She can keep him company." On the appointed day, I left Sophie and Melville at the animal hospital, went out for some pizza, and returned a few hours later to pick them up. The surgery went fine, but when I brought them home, Sophie's attitude toward her new mate had inexplicably changed. She was no longer interested in his companionship; indeed, she was rather aggressive. "It happens sometimes," the vet told me. "The stress of a hospital visit can cause an upset." This was more than an upset; this was a breakup, and no matter what I tried, I couldn't get them to re-bond.

With a new dynamic in the house, I rearranged the living room so that Melville and Sophie had separate quarters. Of course, I couldn't just paint a line down the middle of the room, so I linked an assortment of large exercise pens that gave each rabbit their own space with a safety zone between; they could take turns running through the apartment when I was home to supervise, and I would alternate spending time with them. This arrangement worked fine for months. Then, sadly but not unexpectedly, Melville died. I grieved for this fragile little rabbit, yet I was glad to have given him some joy.

Now it was just Sophie and me, though that would soon change, as I had begun a relationship with a wonderful and deeply compassionate woman named Lauren who shared my abiding love of animals. In the meantime, Sophie had the run of the place, and we got to know each other better. According to Marcy, Sophie had evidently been mistreated by a man, so I didn't think she would be terribly fond of me; I had adopted her because she'd bonded with Melville, though I certainly loved her, too. After a few attempts at finding her another mate, I reckoned Sophie might be happier as a single rabbit. To my surprise, she grew close to me, and again I was reminded of a rabbit's capacity for trusting and forgiving humanity.

As she became more comfortable, Sophie was not shy about expressing her likes and dislikes. She didn't mind the vacuum cleaner, for instance, but the sound of the salad spinner would send her running for cover into the farthest reaches of the apartment. In particular, she was adept at picking up and hurling nearly any object that she wanted to out of her personal space, often accompanied by a short grunt, which is the bunny way of complaining. And what she could not pick up she gnawed on. A toy she was bored with? Flung away. A magazine I'd carelessly left on the couch? Nibbled to confetti. One of my running shoes? Goodbye, laces. What she loved more than anything, though, was affection, and I was only too pleased to heap it upon her. I would softly stroke the top of her head with my fingers or pet the length of her back with my palm, and she would close her eyes and grind her teeth in contentment. She learned to enjoy the attention so much that she would seek me out, nudging my feet with her nose or positioning her head beneath my hand.

Once Lauren and I moved in together, we rented a much larger flat with more room for Sophie to explore and play. One of the stories Lauren likes to tell about Sophie takes place as she was leaving our apartment to go to work. She had packed a canvas bag with some food for lunch, slid one arm through the handles, then kneeled to say goodbye to Sophie, who rushed toward her, resting her front paws on her thigh. Lauren was elated by this unexpected display of affection—until Sophie reached over her shoulder to grab the banana peeking out of the bag! Sophie was loaded with personality, and according to Lauren, she was able to sense when I was about to come home from work, which was almost always the same time. Apparently, after an afternoon of mischievous antics, she would run to her blanket near the front door, smooth it out with her forepaws, and relax as if to say, "I've been here all day behaving myself, and I'd like a few dried cranberries with my dinner."

Lauren and I do not currently live with any animals; we travel frequently and found the heartache of losing Sophie (in 2013) and other four-legged companions a bit too much to bear. But we relish spending time with friends who have adopted rabbits or when we can visit sanctuaries where rescued rabbits live. Their playful nature reminds me not to take life too seriously.

Quite often they come to me in my dreams—rabbits I have known and loved who tell me through the mystical distance that they are well. They sometimes greet me in these visions with the same exuberant dance they used to express pleasure on Earth: the hopping, twisting, gymnastic binky that has come to symbolize the happy rabbit. We are always overjoyed to see one another, though I confess that at times these dreams make me sad, because they accentuate my grief over having lost them. A therapist recently suggested that by communicating with me in my subconscious these former companions are perhaps trying to take care of *me* as I once took care of *them*. Lauren put it another way. "They are giving you love," she said.

For me, being in the company of a rabbit, especially in a space where they feel safe, is invigorating. With their whimsical behavior and intrinsic mindfulness, they exemplify the spirit of living in the moment while also enjoying complex inner lives. I appreciate that although rabbits around the world share many qualities—the herbivorous diet, the fastidious grooming, the ability to locate and bite through your most expensive charging cords—each is a unique individual with personality traits and a temperament all their own. I respect their will and allow them to decide when they'd like to be petted (well, I usually do). Being in their presence is like watching poetry.

More than anything, though, I feel an inexpressible connection with them. This may sound strange, but sometimes it's as if I am one of them. Maybe it is because they are quiet and have a sweet tooth or that for them nothing is as refreshing as napping beneath an open window on a warm day. Perhaps the naturalist Ronald Lockley put it best. "Rabbits are so human," he wrote. "Or is it the other way round—humans are so rabbit?"

Appendix A

Ten Ways You Can Help Rabbits

1. Treat wild rabbits with kindness. If your yard or garden is overrun with rabbits eating your flowers and vegetables, seek humane solutions. Planting onions may keep rabbits away, since they dislike the smell. Consider landscaping with plants that rabbits don't particularly care for, such as allium, anise hyssop, bee balm, catmint, daffodils, ice plant, juniper, peonies, and yarrow. Also, strong fencing can help protect your garden.

2. Watch out for nests. Not all rabbits burrow safely underground, so before mowing your lawn, carefully check the grass—and watch for patches of brown (dead) grass, which may indicate a camouflaged nest near the ground surface. Baby rabbits grow up fast, and the family will likely be gone within a few weeks.

3. Volunteer at your local shelter or rabbit rescue organization. There is plenty to do: socialize the rabbits, clean their cages, bring them hay and veggies, and do whatever they need to keep them healthy and happy and to make them more adoptable. (You may need to attend a training session to be a shelter volunteer.)

4. Adopt, don't shop. If you decide a companion rabbit is right for you, adopt one (or more) from a local animal shelter or rabbit rescue group rather than buying one. You'll save a life and discourage rabbit breeding.

5. Do not give rabbits as Easter presents. Every year, well-meaning parents give rabbits to their children, believing bunnies are a great "starter pet." They don't understand that rabbits need special care and can live a decade or longer.

6. Make companion animals part of the family. Don't relegate a rabbit to a backyard hutch or cage. These are affectionate, playful animals who deserve to live with you indoors, where they are safe from predators and inclement weather.

7. Do not disturb young rabbits you think are "orphaned." Mother rabbits often leave their babies alone for long periods of time, and they will return. If you believe a wild rabbit has truly been abandoned, contact a wildlife rescue group.

8. Assist domesticated stray rabbits. If you find an abandoned or lost rabbit who was clearly someone's companion (physical characteristics may include lop ears or fur that is spotted, white, black, or otherwise unlike that of a wild rabbit), carefully catch them. Capturing a skittish rabbit can require several people and a great deal of patience but leaving out some water and food—such as leafy greens and sliced banana—can help. Once the rabbit is safe, contact your local rabbit rescue organization or animal shelter.

9. Do not participate in rabbit exploitation: don't wear their fur, eat them, or use products tested on animals.

10. Support rescue nonprofits. There are numerous organizations that either rehabilitate wild rabbits and other wildlife or find homes for companion rabbits. Most of these groups rely on the financial support of donors. An online search will direct you to one in your area, or you can choose to contribute to a national organization, such as the House Rabbit Society in the USA, the Rabbit Welfare Association & Fund in the UK, or the Rabbit Run-Away Orphanage in Australia, among many others.

Appendix B

Recommended Reading

Unlike books about dogs and cats, there is a regrettable shortage of nonfiction books focusing on rabbits and our relationship with them. Here are some you might enjoy.

Susan Davis and Margo DeMello, *Stories Rabbits Tell: A Natural and Cultural History of a Misunderstood Creature*, 2003. (Includes a comprehensive look at how rabbits are exploited.)

Victoria Dickenson, *Rabbit*, 2014.

Marinell Harriman, *House Rabbit Handbook: How to Live with an Urban Rabbit*, 5th Edition, 2013. (Periodically revised.)

R. M. Lockley, *The Private Life of the Rabbit: An Account of the Life History and Social Behavior of the Wild Rabbit*, 1964. (This out-of-print book is actually science, not social, but it's worth a look. You can find a copy for sale online.)

Susan Lumpkin and John Seidensticker, *Rabbits: The Animal Answer Guide*, 2011.

Marie Mead and Nancy LaRoche, *Rabbits: Gentle Hearts, Valiant Spirits*, 2007.

Lucile Moore and Kathy Smith, *Touched by a Rabbit: A Treasury of Stories about Rabbits and Their People*, 2009.

Barbara Purchase, *Rabbit Tales*, 1982. (Also out of print, though used copies can be found.)

Cecil S. Webb, *A Hare About the House*, 1955. (Yet another out-of-print book you might find for sale online.)

Endnotes

Introduction

believed both the females and males could give birth: John Sheail, *Rabbits and Their History* (David & Charles Limited, 1971), p. 22.

"There are not many stories": Harrison William Weir, *Harrison Weir's Pictures of Birds and Other Family Pets* (Religious Tract Society, 1879), n.p.

"It does not appear possible": Jane Loudon, *Domestic Pets: Their Habits and Management* (Grant and Griffith, 1851), p. 61.

"the most foolish": Charles Kingsley, *The Boys' and Girls' Book of Science* (Strahan and Company Limited, 1881), p. 338.

"odd, quaint, and ludicrous beings": John George Wood, *Wood's Animal Kingdom Illustrated* (H. A. Brown & Company, 1870), p. 584.

"As a rule": Mathilde Sandras, *Snowdrop: Or the Adventures of a White Rabbit* (T. Nelson and Sons, 1873), p. v.

his colleagues worried: Irene M. Pepperberg, "In Memoriam: Donald R. Griffin, 1915–2003," *The Auk*, Volume 123, Number 2, April 1, 2006, p. 596.

Chapter One: Habitat and Conservation

Master Rabbit I saw: Excerpted from "As I Was Walking," Walter de la Mare, *Poems: 1919 to 1934* (Constable and Company Limited, 1935), p. 293.

Barrett suspected: Email from Jonathan Barrett, son of Aubrey Barrett, January 16, 2020.

"I think this might be a rabbit": https://www.atlasobscura.com/articles/found-britains-first-pet-bunny

caught fire sometime between 270 and 280: George Balcombe, *History of Building: Styles, Methods, and Materials* (Batsford Academic and Educational, 1985), p. 19.

Field of the Fallen Hall: Richard Jones, "Names and Archaeology," from *The Oxford Handbook of Names and Naming*, edited by Carole Hough (Oxford University Press, 2016), p. 475.

"This is thirty-five million years older": https://www.livescience.com/2381-fossil-oldest-rabbit-relative.html

Dr. Rose told me: Email from Kenneth Rose, January 13, 2020.

impossible to pinpoint: As an example of how these numbers can change, consider that when Susan Davis and Margo DeMello published their excellent book *Stories Rabbits Tell* in 2003, they counted 24 species of rabbits, 29 species of hares, and 25 species of pikas. There are now seven additional species of rabbits, three more species of hares, and another four species of pikas—for now.

rabbits and hares likely originated in Asia: Thomas Lacher, Jordan Rogan, et al., "Evolution, phylogeny, ecology and conservation of the Clade Glires: Lagomorpha and Rodentia," from *Handbook of the Mammals of the World, Volume 6: Lagomorphs and Rodents I*, edited by Don E. Wilson, Thomas E. Lacher, Jr., and Russell A. Mittermeier (Lynx Ediciones, 2016), pp. 15–26.

65 million years ago: Jin Meng and André R. Wyss, "Glires (Lagomorpha, Rodentia)," from *The Rise of Placental Mammals: Origins and Relationships of the Major Extant Clades*, edited by Kenneth D. Rose and J. David Archibald (The Johns Hopkins University Press, 2005), p. 152. I am grateful to Dr. Meng for helping me with the lagomorph timeline.

rabbits and hares are more closely related to primates: https://www.newscientist.com/article/mg14920143-000-meet-brer-rabbit-and-sister-hare/

rabbits probably share: Email from Dr. Polina Perelman, March 27, 2020.

the Roman word for the nation: John A. Crow, *Spain: The Root and the Flower: An Interpretation of Spain and the Spanish People*, Third Edition (University of California Press, 2005), p. 7.

Some biologists speculate: Radu Cornel Guiaşu, *Non-native Species and Their Role in the Environment: The Need for a Broader Perspective* (Brill, 2016), p. 30.

lightkeepers had released: Mandi Johnson, "Deadly rabbit disease confirmed in the San Juans," July 23, 2019, https://www.sanjuanjournal.com/news/deadly-rabbit-disease-confirmed-in-the-san-juans/

By 1924, the digging: David Brian Plummer, *In Pursuit of Coney* (Coch-y-Bonddu Books, 2001), p. 20.

The introduction of a few rabbits: Bill Fawcett, *100 Mistakes That Changed History: Backfires and Blunders That Collapsed Empires, Crashed Economies, and Altered the Course of Our World* (Penguin Publishing Group, 2010), p. 166.

lagomorphs tend to live in temperate zones: Susan Lumpkin and John Seidensticker, *Rabbits: The Animal Answer Guide* (Johns Hopkins University Press, 2011), p. 88.

most animals and plants have been there longer: John J. Wiens, Catherine H. Graham, et al., "Evolutionary and Ecological Causes of the Latitudinal Diversity Gradient in Hylid Frogs: Treefrog Trees Unearth the Roots of High Tropical Diversity," *The American Naturalist*, Volume 168, Number 5, November 2006, pp. 579–96.

a radius of 50 feet (15 m) or more: Lucía Gálvez, Antonio López-Pintor, et al., "Ecosystem Engineering Effects of European Rabbits in a Mediterranean Habitat," from *Lagomorph Biology: Evolution, Ecology, and Conservation*, edited by Paulo C. Alves, Nuno Ferrand, and Klaus Hackländer (Springer, 2008), p. 125.

Dominant rabbits require submissive acts: Louis DiVincenti, Jr., and Angelika N. Rehrig, "The Social Nature of European Rabbits (*Oryctolagus cuniculus*)," *Journal of the American Association for Laboratory Animal Science*, Volume 55, Number 6, November 2016, pp. 729–36.

the female rabbit does most of the digging work: Paul E.

Hatcher and Nick Battey, *Biological Diversity: Exploiters and Exploited* (Wiley-Blackwell, 2011), p. 205.

he may scrape a shallow hole: R. M. Lockley, "Social structure and stress in the rabbit warren," *Journal of Animal Ecology*, Volume 30, Number 2, November 1961, p. 408.

Just which of the two rabbits: Based on email correspondence with Margo DeMello, former president of the House Rabbit Society and coauthor of *Stories Rabbits Tell* (February 11, 2020), as well as biologists Miguel Carneiro (February 12, 2020) and Jorge Lozano (February 13, 2020).

and even hawks: For example, "Rabbit wins battle with hawk," *The Shreveport Times*, June 11, 1965, p. 10.

it is always the female: R. M. Lockley, *The Private Life of the Rabbit* (Andre Deutsch Limited, 1964), p. 135.

Evidence suggests: R. M. Lockley, "Social structure and stress in the rabbit warren," *Journal of Animal Ecology*, Volume 30, Number 2, November 1961, p. 402.

"It all made sense": Interview with Greger Larson, August 10, 2018.

Some of the earliest archeological records: Naomi Sykes and Julie Curl, "The Rabbit," from *Extinctions and Invasions: A Social History of British Fauna*, edited by Terry O'Connor and Naomi Jane Sykes (Oxbow Books, 2010), pp. 118–19.

could have begun in earnest: Evan K. Irving-Pease, Laurent A. F. Frantz, et al., "Rabbits and the specious origins of domestication," *Trends in Ecology and Evolution*, Volume 33, Issue 3, March 1, 2018, pp. 149–52.

The Annamite striped rabbit: Andrew Tilker, An Nguyen, et al., "A little-known endemic caught in the South-east Asian extinction crisis: The Annamite striped rabbit *Nesolagus timminsi*," *Oryx*, 2018, pp. 1–10.

Climate change has left the riverine rabbit: Gregory Hughes, Wilfred Thuiller, et al., "Environmental change hastens the demise of the critically endangered riverine rabbit (*Bunola-*

gus monticularis)," *Biological Conservation*, Volume 141, January 2008, pp. 23–34.

Amami rabbits: https://blogs.scientificamerican.com/extinction-countdown/rare-japanese-rabbit-leaves-endangered-species-list/

the riparian brush rabbit had completely disappeared: https://www.usda.gov/media/blog/2014/12/02/vanished-rabbit-reappears-central-californias-dos-rios-ranch

In Spain, Portugal, and France: https://www.portugalresident.com/rabbit-now-in-danger-of-extinction-along-with-30000-other-animals-birds-and-plants/

fewer than 50 individuals: https://www.fws.gov/wafwo/articles.cfm?id=149489590

some 2000 rabbits: Carl Segerstrom, "After nearly going extinct, Washington's pygmy rabbits need room to grow," *High Country News*, May 31, 2019, https://www.hcn.org/issues/51.10/endangered-species-after-nearly-going-extinct-washingtons-pygmy-rabbits-need-room-to-grow

"Local people have great power": https://www.edgeofexistence.org/blog/the-power-of-community-the-volcano-rabbit/

"We follow safety guidelines": Email from Eileen McGourty, February 10, 2020.

seemed to avoid the snakes altogether: Fumio Yamada, "A Review of the Biology and Conservation of the Amami Rabbit (*Pentalagus furnessi*)," from *Lagomorph Biology: Evolution, Ecology, and Conservation*, edited by Paulo C. Alves, Nuno Ferrand, and Klaus Hackländer (Springer, 2008), p. 374.

The situation has greatly improved for the Amami rabbits: Masahiko Ohta, "Amami rabbit numbers revived after removal of mongooses," *The Asahi Shimbun*, April 10, 2109, http://www.asahi.com/ajw/articles/AJ201904100001.html

It was the farmers' children and wives: Margo DeMello, 2010, "Becoming rabbit: Living with and knowing rabbits," *Spring: A Journal of Archetype and Culture*, Volume 83, pp. 237–52.

Chapter Two: Leporine Lore

"For am I not the biggest": Anita Yasuda, *Stolen Fire: A Seminole Trickster Myth* (Magic Wagon, 2013), p. 22.

rabbits had the ability to observe everything: Susan E. Davis and Margo DeMello, *Stories Rabbits Tell: A Natural and Cultural History of a Misunderstood Creature* (Lantern, 2003), p. 132.

the hare was sacred to Aphrodite: August Heinrich Petiscus, *The Gods of Olympos: Or, Mythology of the Greeks and Romans* (T. Fisher Unwin, 1892), p. 96.

a hare or rabbit could portend: *Encyclopedia of Superstitions, Folklore, and the Occult Sciences of the World*, Volume II, edited by Cora Linn Daniels and C. M. Stevans (University Press of the Pacific, 1971), p. 13.

another example of misfortune: Barbara Purchase, *Rabbit Tales* (Van Nostrand Reinhold Company, 1982), p. 112.

hares seemed to have: Barbara Clay Finch, "Some Small Deer," from *The Monthly Packet*, Volume XCVI, edited by Christabel R. Coleridge and Arthur Innes (A. D. Innes Company, Limited, 1898), pp. 68–9.

In a Tibetan version: "How the Rabbit Killed the Lion," from *Tibetan Folk Tales*, translated by A. L. Shelton (Abela Publishing, 2009), pp. 65–7.

linked to the explorer John Colter: *Encyclopedia of Deception*, edited by Timothy R. Levine (SAGE, 2014), p. 555.

a couple of Wyoming taxidermists: *American Folklore: An Encyclopedia*, edited by Jan Harold Brunvand (Garland Publishing, Inc., 1996), p. 831.

the rabbit even shakes free the insects: Ken and Visakha Kawasaki, *Jataka Tales of the Buddha: An Anthology, Volume II* (Pariyatti Press, 2018), p. 117.

the Roman dictator Julius Caesar: he wrote about hares in his work *Commentarii de Bello Gallico* ("Commentaries on the

Gallic War").

Chapter Three: The Legacy of Eostre

sacred animal is said to be a rabbit: Martin Greif, *The Holiday Book: America's Festivals and Celebrations* (Universe Books, 1978), p. 84.

Some authors have claimed: Rob Cowen, *Common Ground: Encounters with Nature at the Edges of Life* (University of Chicago Press, 2015), p. 89.

"Eostre's totem animal": Kerr Cuhulain, *Pagan Religions: A Handbook for Diversity Training* (Acorn Guild Press, 2011), p. 102.

An intriguing point about the link between Eostre and hares: Naomi Sykes, *Beastly Questions: Animal Answers to Archaeological Issues* (Bloomsbury, 2014), p. 90.

Venerable Bede: See *Bede: The Reckoning of Time*, translated by Faith Wallis (Liverpool University Press, 1999), p. 54.

"All the stuff about dawn and hares": Email from Martha Bayless, April 3, 2020.

"First the great nineteenth-century German scholar": Email from Ronald Hutton, April 3, 2020.

"He likely did this": https://blogs.loc.gov/folklife/2016/04/ostara-and-the-hare/

Charles Billson observed: Charles J. Billson, "The Easter Hare," *Folk-Lore*, Volume 3, Number 4 (December 1892), Taylor & Francis, Ltd. on behalf of Folklore Enterprises Ltd.

"What we're trying to show": Interview with Naomi Sykes, January 9, 2019.

"He didn't start out as a bunny": Interview with Luke John Murphy, January 4, 2019.

"We don't really know": Interview with Philip A. Shaw, September 4, 2018.

One possible explanation: https://ahrc-blog.com/2020/04/10/the-fable-of-britains-easter-animals/

"**incredible cultural connection**": Interview with Carly Ameen, September 27, 2018.

"**never really been studied using archeology**": Interview with Thomas Fowler, January 10, 2019.

a practice Jacob Grimm wrote about: Jacob Grimm, *Deutsche Mythologie* (Dieterichschen Buchhandlung, 1835), p. 182. The specific phrase is *Freudenfeuer wurden zu Ostern angezündet* ("bonfires were lighted at Easter").

"**on Easter morning it is the duty and pleasure**": *Belmont Chronicle*, March 29, 1877, p. 2.

Easter-bunny: "About Easter Eggs," *Liverpool Echo*, April 3, 1893, p. 4.

puffins and shearwaters have been known to evict rabbits: John Sheail, *Rabbits and Their History* (David & Charles Limited, 1971), p. 30.

1890 article: "The decay of Easter," *The Scots Observer: A Record and Review, Volume III*, April 12, 1890, p. 577.

"**In Alsace and neighboring regions**": Adapted from the translation by Stephen Winick at https://blogs.loc.gov/folklife/2016/03/easter-bunny/

7 percent of adults: Elisabeth Sherman, "Survey finds that too many people still think chocolate milk comes from brown cows," FoodandWine.com, June 1, 2017, foodandwine.com/news/survey-finds-too-many-people-still-think-chocolate-milk-comes-brown-cows

Chapter Four: Lagomorph Lexicon and Literature

Once upon a time: Beatrix Potter, *The Tale of Peter Rabbit* (Frederick Warne & Co., 1902).

"**For a hare was believed**": Pamela Hopkins, "The White Rabbit?" *The Pilgrim Rabbit*, February 2019, pp. 2–3.

the author sent Tenniel: "Down the rabbit hole with St. Mary's Church," *Just Beverley*, Issue 3, March 1, 2015, p. 14.

about 600 years: Gerald E. H. Barrett-Hamilton, *A History of*

British Mammals, Volume 2 (Gurney and Jackson, 1910), p. 177.

the word "conigrave": Naomi Sykes and Julie Curl, "The Rabbit," from *Extinctions and Invasions: A Social History of British Fauna*, edited by Terry O'Connor and Naomi Jane Sykes (Oxbow Books, 2010), p. 121.

English fondness for slang: https://www.etymonline.com/word/coney

by the 1800s: Keith Allan and Kate Burridge, *Forbidden Words: Taboo and the Censoring of Language* (Cambridge University Press, 2002), p. 44.

Coney Island was so named: *America's Changing Neighborhoods: An Exploration of Diversity through Places*, edited by Reed Ueda (Greenwood, 2017), p. 412.

Coneyhurst definition: David Mills, *A Dictionary of British Place-Names* (Oxford University Press, 2011), p. 127.

Conies Down, Conisholme Cross, Conegar Hill, Coney Bury, and Conies Dale definitions: Courtesy of the English Place-Name Society, http://epns.nottingham.ac.uk/

Knocknagoney Down definition: David Mills, *A Dictionary of British Place-Names* (Oxford University Press, 2011), p. 282.

Coneythorpe definition: David Mills, *A Dictionary of British Place-Names* (Oxford University Press, 2011), p. 127.

Anatoly Liberman addresses 55 words: Anatoly Liberman, *An Analytic Dictionary of English Etymology: An Introduction* (University of Minnesota Press, 2008), pp. 176–80.

Bunny definition: Caroline Taggart, *The Book of English Place Names: How Our Towns and Villages Got Their Names* (Ebury Publishing, 2011), p. 126.

"my love, my dove": *The Origin of the English Drama*, Volume 3, edited by Thomas Hawkins (Clarendon Press, 1773), p. 317.

"My two daughters": *Notes and Queries*, Tenth Series, Volume XI, January–June, 1909, pp. 208 and 258.

"Even Mr. [Franklin] Roosevelt": "Strange superstitions," *The Nottingham Evening Post*, November 27, 1935, p. 10.

comedian Gilda Radner: Alan Zweibel, *Bunny Bunny: Gilda Radner—A Sort of Love Story* (1997), pp. 106–7.

"a more complex fellow": Douglas Martin, "Ronald Lockley, of rabbit fame, dies at 96," *The New York Times*, April 24, 2000, Section A, p. 24.

"wuffy, fluffy": Richard Adams, *Watership Down* (Scribner, 2005), p. xiv.

"It's just a story about rabbits": Mark Brown, "'True meaning' of *Watership Down* revealed ahead of TV revival," *The Guardian*, December 10, 2018.

"contributed several good suggestions": Richard Adams, *Watership Down* (Scribner, 2005), p. xiii.

"These stories are true": Ernest Thompson Seton, *Wild Animals I Have Known* (Dover Edition, 2000), p. 7.

rabbits have no speech as we understand it: Ernest Thompson Seton, *Wild Animals I Have Known* (Dover Edition, 2000), pp. 71–2.

"As soon as Rag was big enough": Ernest Thompson Seton, *Wild Animals I Have Known* (Dover Edition, 2000), p. 82.

Interesting side note about Seton: When he turned 21, his father, an accountant, presented him with an itemized bill for the cost of raising him, including the doctor's fee for his delivery. Seton supposedly paid the bill, which totaled $537.50 plus 6 percent interest, and never spoke to his father again. See David Graeber, *Debt: The First 5,000 Years* (Melville House, 2011), p. 92.

"There are no stories of animal intelligence": John Burroughs, "Real and Sham Natural History," *The Wild Animal Story*, edited by Ralph H. Lutts (Temple University Press, 1998), p. 132.

Declining in popularity: Lily West, "Differences Between Victorian & Edwardian Fashion," https://www.leaf.tv/articles/differences-between-victorian-edwardian-fashion/

Mr. Rabbit Trick: Stephen King, *On Writing: A Memoir of the*

Craft (Scribner, 2000), pp. 28–9.

"The public must be fond of rabbits!": Linda Lear, *Beatrix Potter: A Life in Nature* (St. Martin's Griffin, 2007), p. 152.

she presaged the era of product merchandising: Beatrix Potter was not the first author to merchandise her work, but she created a successful product line through a combination of legal protection and marketing instinct. As *Smithsonian* magazine put it, "In modern terms, she created a brand out of her artistic work—an approach that has been imitated ever since." See Joy Lanzendorfer, "How Beatrix Potter Invented Character Merchandising," January 31, 2017, smithsonianmag.com/arts-culture/how-beatrix-potter-invented-character-merchandising-180961979/

In her book *The Case of Peter Rabbit*: Margaret Mackey, *The Case of Peter Rabbit: Changing Conditions of Literature for Children* (Taylor & Francis e-Library, 2005), pp. 35–67.

"All outward forms of religion": Clifford M. Reed, "Beatrix Potter's Unitarian Context," from *Beatrix Potter: Thirty Years of Discovery and Appreciation*, edited by Libby Joy and Judy Taylor (Beatrix Potter Society, 2010), p. 161.

The Rabbit Scribe: Erik Velásquez García, "Reflections on the Codex Style and the Princeton Vessel," *The PARI Journal*, Volume X, No. 1, Summer 2009, p. 10.

ran on three different New York stages: According to the Thornton W. Burgess Research League, http://twbresearchleague.blogspot.com/2010/03/peter-rabbit-in-dreamland_07.html

"This news of Georgie's": Robert Lawson, *Rabbit Hill* (Puffin Modern Classics, 1977), p. 12.

"I don't know what good it did them": *Newbery Medal Books, 1922–1955*, Volume 1, edited by Bertha Mahony Miller and Elinor Whitney Field (The Horn Book, 1955), p. 266.

"Well, there's Little Georgie": *Newbery Medal Books, 1922–1955*, Volume 1, edited by Bertha Mahony Miller and Elinor Whitney Field (The Horn Book, 1955), p. 266.

"I pushed the pencil and pecked at the typewriter": *Newbery Medal Books, 1922–1955*, Volume 1, edited by Bertha Mahony Miller and Elinor Whitney Field (The Horn Book, 1955), p. 265.

nurture compassion for animals: Monica Flegel, "Mistresses as Masters: Voicing Female Power Through the Subject Animal in Two Nineteenth-Century Animal Autobiographies," from *Speaking for Animals: Animal Autobiographical Writing*, edited by Margo DeMello (Routledge, 2013), p. 90.

"Good deeds are worth more": Mathilde Sandras, *Snowdrop: Or the Adventures of a White Rabbit* (T. Nelson and Sons, 1873), p. 95.

"It is very cruel to amuse oneself": Mathilde Sandras, *Snowdrop: Or the Adventures of a White Rabbit* (T. Nelson and Sons, 1873), p. 151.

"Why cannot each animal be content": Mathilde Sandras, *Snowdrop: Or the Adventures of a White Rabbit* (T. Nelson and Sons, 1873), p. 217.

"A Rabbit as King of the Ghosts": *The Palm at the End of the Mind: Selected Poems and a Play by Wallace Stevens*, edited by Holly Stevens (Vintage Books, 1990), pp. 150–1.

others propose that Stevens: See Edward Ragg, *Wallace Stevens and the Aesthetics of Abstraction* (Cambridge University Press, 2010), p. 15.

"I spend the time worrying about the rabbit": Wallace Stevens, *Letters of Wallace Stevens*, edited by Holly Stevens (University of California Press, 1966), p. 321.

"Song of the Rabbits Outside the Tavern": *The Oxford Illustrated Book of American Children's Poems*, edited by Donald Hall (Oxford University Press, 2001), p. 50.

"Hares at Play": John Clare, *Selected Poems*, edited by Geoffrey Summerfield (Penguin Books, 1990), pp. 117–18.

Chapter Five: Rabbits in Art

"Rabbits speak to me in spirit": Interview with Hunt Slonem, June 19, 2019.

It took just ten minutes: Meera Dolasia, "American Artist Jeff Koons' 'Rabbit' Sculpture Auctions for a Record $91 Million," https://www.dogonews.com/2019/5/19/american-artist-jeff-koons-rabbit-sculpture-auctions-for-a-record-91-dollars-million. It was later revealed that Robert Mnuchin purchased the work for the billionaire hedge fund manager Steven A. Cohen.

Artnet News called the work: https://news.artnet.com/market/christies-contemporary-auction-may-2019-1545007

"taps into the visual language of childhood": https://www.christies.com/features/Jeff-Koons-Rabbit-Own-the-controversy-9804-3.aspx

"I feel that the reason": Email from Dr. Sue Andrew, February 17, 2020.

in a 1993 study: Peter Brugger and Susan Brugger, "The Easter Bunny in October: Is It Disguised as a Duck?," *Perceptual and Motor Skills, 76*, April 1993, pp. 557–8.

"An artwork as precious and irreplaceable": Email from Christof Metzger, February 14, 2020.

"The rabbit is the only animal that is present": Elisabeth Delahaye, *The Lady and the Unicorn* (Réunion des Musées Nationaux, 2007), p. 69.

"she broke her leg in a miserable manner": *The Caledonian Mercury*, August 5, 1736, p. 3.

Potter scholar Joyce Irene Whalley contends: Joyce Irene Whalley, "Beatrix Potter's Art," from *Beatrix Potter's Peter Rabbit: A Children's Classic at 100*, edited by Margaret Mackey (Scarecrow Press, Inc., 2002), p. 46.

Caldecott was also important to her: Email from Libby Joy of The Beatrix Potter Society, July 13, 2020.

As Potter biographer Linda Lear observes: Linda Lear, *Beatrix*

Potter: A Life in Nature (St. Martin's Griffin, 2007), pp. 154–5.

So adamant was Beatrix Potter: Tess Cosslett, *Talking Animals in British Children's Fiction, 1786–1914* (Routledge, 2016), p. 172.

painted the portrait of a ghost so realistically: Walters Museum of Art, https://art.thewalters.org/detail/32308/yoshi-toshi-ryakuga/

Choju-giga: https://e.kyoto-np.jp/news/20140707/919.html

her husband Garry told me: Email from Garry Keay, June 12, 2019.

"I'll choose a subject": Email from Sam Cannon, June 22, 2019.

two of them in a backyard hutch: Jessica Cohen, "Bunnies hop into high art at Hotel Fauchere," *The Times Herald-Record*, April 19, 2019.

"Their names were Pixie and Barnaby": Interview with Hunt Slonem, June 19, 2019.

remind the viewer: http://www.jimon.com/artists/hunt-slonem/

one legend says: Barbara Hodgson, "The stories behind Newcastle's so-called 'Vampire Rabbit,'" *Chronicle Live*, January 15, 2017, https://www.chroniclelive.co.uk/news/north-east-news/stories-behind-newcastles-called-vampie-12455793

the Berlin Wall Memorial lists 140: https://www.berliner-mauer-gedenkstaette.de/en/todesopfer-240.html

The rabbits enjoyed a generally peaceful life: *Rabbit à la Berlin* (2009), documentary directed by Bartosz Konopka.

Most of the leporine Berliners migrated west: Geoffrey Macnab, "Rabbits in Berlin's death zone," *The Guardian*, March 11, 2010, https://www.theguardian.com/film/2010/mar/11/rabbit-a-la-berlin

"I always knew": Email from Karla Sachse, February 22, 2020.

"The reference to rabbits": https://www.berlin.de/mauer/en/sites/artistic-markers/kaninchenfeld-rabbit-field-karla-sachse-1999-481548.en.php

"There are only about sixty figures left": Email from Karla

Sachse, February 22, 2020.

the organic process of decay: Sarah Suzuki, *Wait, Later This Will Be Nothing: Editions by Dieter Roth* (The Museum of Modern Art, 2012), p. 26.

Chapter Six: Rabbits in Popular Culture

"Hallo, Rabbit": A. A. Milne, *The Complete Tales of Winnie-the-Pooh* (Dutton Children's Books, 1992), p. 112.

Oswald the Lucky Rabbit was a huge hit: David A. Bossert, *Oswald the Lucky Rabbit: The Search for the Lost Disney Cartoons* (Disney Editions, 2017), p. 18.

required more Plasticine: https://www.guinnessworldrecords. com/world-records/most-plasticine-used-in-a-feature-film

"He's a little stinker": Peter B. Flint, "Mel Blanc, who provided voices for 3,000 cartoons, is dead at 81," *The New York Times*, July 11, 1989, Section A, p. 16.

"Bugs Bunny is definitely": Email from Christopher P. Lehman, July 7, 2020.

Bugs Bunny's lineage: Christopher P. Lehman, *The Colored Cartoon: Black Representation in American Animated Short Films, 1907–1954* (University of Massachusetts Press, 2007), pp. 64–5.

"has nothing but pleasant memories": Joel Chandler Harris, *Uncle Remus: His Songs and Sayings* (D. Appleton and Company, 1898), p. xvii.

"fairly offensive": Paul Bond, "Iger keeping options open for ABC," HollywoodReporter.com, March 10, 2010, https:// www.hollywoodreporter.com/news/iger-keeping-options-open-abc-21512

The inspiration for this cinematic moment: Dianne Scillia, "Hunter Rabbits/Hares in Fifteenth- and Sixteenth-Century Northern European Art: Parody and Carnival?" from *Parody and Festivity in Early Modern Art: Essays on Comedy as Social Vision*, edited by David R. Smith (Ashgate Publishing Company, 2012), p. 46.

"the reversal of normality": Email from Christopher de Hamel, February 14, 2020.

"You just want to burst out laughing": Michelangelo Capua, *Janet Leigh: A Biography* (McFarland & Company, Inc., 2013), p. 134.

"I've forgotten as much as I could": Tom Weaver, "Janet Leigh: Mistress of Menace," *Starlog*, Issue 132, July 1988, p. 16.

He said he approached *Us*: Kevin Polowy, "Jordan Peele explains the meaning of rabbits in 'Us,' says it's an Easter movie," *Yahoo Entertainment*, June 18, 2019, https://www.yahoo.com/entertainment/us-easter-movie-rabbits-jordan-peele-130000385.html

"rabbit love is inappropriate": Kate Wright, *Transdisciplinary Journeys in the Anthropocene: More-Than-Human Encounters* (Routledge, 2017), p. 126.

"wholehearted admiration for our rabbits": "Aussie artist aids rabbits," *Lubbock Evening Journal*, July 23, 1954, p. 22.

"a rabbit was about as Australian": Lynne Bell, "A rabbit paid the fares," *The Sydney Morning Herald*, December 12, 1968, p. 28.

"a sturdy, kindly little person": "A tale of two rabbits: The hero and the pest," *The Sydney Morning Herald*, December 12, 1953, p. 2.

many of whom sent letters to the paper: "Obituaries: Nan Fullarton," *The Sydney Morning Herald*, May 4, 2000, p. 32.

least of all Australia's farmers: "Obituaries: Nan Fullarton," *The Sydney Morning Herald*, May 4, 2000, p. 32.

"The most peculiar thing I have seen in Australia": "A tale of two rabbits: The hero and the pest," *The Sydney Morning Herald*, December 12, 1953, p. 2.

"Miss Nan Fullarton's Frisky would poll well": "PE(S)T in the public eye: Rabbits lay pink eggs," *The Sun-Herald*, April 18, 1954, p. 14.

"Rabbits must be one of the most likable pests": "A tale of two rabbits: The hero and the pest," *The Sydney Morning Herald*, December 12, 1953, p. 2.

the couple decided that a rabbit: James Howe, "Introduction to the 40th-Anniversary Edition of Bunnicula," from *Bunnicula: A Tale of Rabbit Mystery* (Atheneum, 2019), p. xii. Sadly, Deborah died of cancer before the first Bunnicula book was published.

"Besides," James Howe later recalled: James Howe, "Writing Bunnicula: The Story Behind the Story," https://www.jameshowe.com/writing-bunnicula

"The truth is": https://www.amherst.edu/amherst-story/magazine/extra/node/66410

Faith McNulty wrote: Faith McNulty, "Children's Books for Christmas," *The New Yorker*, December 6, 1982, p. 180.

"both children and their toys": Allan Kellehear, PhD, "Death and Renewal in *The Velveteen Rabbit*: A Sociological Reading," *Journal of Near-Death Studies*, Volume 12, Number 1, Fall 1993, p. 45.

Chapter Seven: Lagomorphs in History

With a finer understanding of Napoleonic strategy: David G. Chandler, *The Campaigns of Napoleon: The Mind and Method of History's Greatest Soldier*, Volume 1 (Scribner, 1966), p. 594.

"My guess is that the rabbit had been startled": *Public Papers of the Presidents of the United States, Jimmy Carter, 1979, Book II—June 23 to December 31, 1979* (United States Government Printing Office, 1980), p. 1579.

some historians say thousands: R. F. Delderfield, *Napoleon's Marshals* (Cooper Square Press, 2002), p. 105.

rabbits raced toward Napoleon: David G. Chandler, *The Campaigns of Napoleon: The Mind and Method of History's Greatest Soldier*, Volume 1 (Scribner, 1966), p. 593.

Napoleon learned that rather than catching wild rabbits: Général de Division Baron Paul-Charles-François-Adrien-Henri Dieudonné Thiébault and Arthur John Butler, *The Memoirs of Baron Thiébault (Late Lieutenant-General in the French Army)* — *Vol. II* (Pickle Partners Publishing, 2013), p. 109.

"Thinking himself surrounded by a thousand devils": Reverend James Hall, *Travels in Scotland by an Unusual Route*, Vol. I (J. Johnson, 1807), p. 168.

"By God, gentlemen": *The Philadelphia Gazette*, June 7, 1733, p. 2.

"Keep him away from the cops": Jeff Guinn, *Go Down Together: The True, Untold Story of Bonnie and Clyde* (Simon & Schuster, 2009), p. 299. Well-armed police would catch up with Bonnie and Clyde a month later and abruptly terminate their crime spree.

"Owing to the warning of the rabbits": "Rabbits save six lives," *Dundee Evening Telegraph*, July 26, 1912, p. 4.

In a similar fashion: "Rabbit saves family," *The News-Messenger*, August 1, 1932, p. 10.

neighbors heard the squeals: "Scared rabbit saves baby!" *The Honolulu Advertiser*, October 1, 1951, p. 3.

dwarf bunny named Radar: "Hero rabbit saves owners from fire," *The Daily Spectrum*, July 3, 1984, p. 18.

"He's just sort of an inside pet": Bonnie Malkin, "Rabbit saves owners from house fire," *The Telegraph*, July 24, 2008, https://www.telegraph.co.uk/news/worldnews/australiaandthepacific/australia/2452505/Rabbit-saves-owners-from-house-fire.html

"My bunnies are my lifesavers": https://www.kold.com/story/24245546/bunnies-to-the-rescue-how-two-rabbits-saved-their-family/

kindhearted Josef Frischauf: "Rescued rabbit saves family," *Santa Maria Times*, February 18, 1960, p. 5.

Blazer climbed the small stairs that gave her access to the couple's bed: Jerry Slavin, "Rabbit saves N.J. couple from deadly gas leak," November 17, 2013, http://skewnews.com/rabbit-saves-n-j-couple-from-deadly-gas-leak/#.XbzMjr97lPM

Dory, who in 2004: "Rabbit saves diabetic from coma," http://news.bbc.co.uk/2/hi/uk_news/england/cambridgesh-ire/3441337.stm

"Victoria told me later": Jennifer S. Holland, *Unlikely Heroes: 37 Inspiring Stories of Courage and Heart from the Animal Kingdom* (Workman Publishing, 2014), pp. 211–12.

the first-ever honorary animal member: "Life-saving rabbit wins top award," http://news.bbc.co.uk/2/hi/uk_news/england/cambridgeshire/3535655.stm

"She was going wild": Jennifer Wulff, "Superpets!" *People*, September 4, 2006, https://people.com/archive/superpets-vol-66-no-10/

"I guess the rabbit was telling her husband": Amy Thon, "Family says rabbit saved woman's life," *Burlington Hawk Eye*, August 16, 2005, p. 2.

"Robin was the reason": Jennifer Wulff, "Superpets!" *People*, September 4, 2006, https://people.com/archive/superpets-vol-66-no-10/

GOAL!: "Rabbit was soccer hero," *The Canberra Times*, September 27, 1960, p. 23.

a man named Clyde: "A man's life saved by a rabbit," *St. Neots Chronicle and Advertiser*, January 30, 1875, p. 4.

"The car was settling down further into the creek": "Train bringing 25th engineers here goes into Nebraska creek," *San Francisco Chronicle*, June 2, 1919, p. 1. Note: the article reports dozens of men were injured, but none died.

"He once woke me up": http://jproc.ca/haida/mascots.html

Handy Built was adopted: Karleen Bradford, *Animal Heroes* (Scholastic Inc., 1995), p. 90.

Acting as a mascot on another warship: Associated Press, "Seaman discards gas mask to save rabbit at Midway," *Evening Star*, July 24, 1942, p. A-7.

Saxon was soon stationed: Chris Watts, "The story of Thomas L. J. Saxon," *Columbian Progress*, January 10, 2009, p. 8.

"These little pets were made": "Defends her love for pet rabbit in reply to pastor," *The Washington Times*, November 3, 1911, p. 19.

"He hops about the hotel": "Has but one ear," *Waterbury Democrat*, July 13, 1896, p. 6.

"the bunny with brains": "Rabbit that takes tea," *New Zealand Herald*, December 17, 1910, p. 2.

A rabbit named Wilfred: "King buys half a rabbit," *Mt. Benger Mail*, September 29, 1926, p. 2.

When Wilfred died: United Press, "King remembers unlucky rabbit," *The Indianapolis Times*, April 22, 1927, p. 24.

Princess Mary: "Had varied taste in pets," *News and Citizen*, September 7, 1921, p. 3.

Princesses Elizabeth and Margaret: "Princesses' pets," *Yorkshire Evening Post*, February 14, 1938, p. 6.

Prince Charles: "Royal rabbit leading 'the life of Riley,'" *The Noblesville Ledger*, October 11, 1954, p. 1.

"When the photographer heard": "Joe, the Pet Rabbit," *Shields Gazette and Daily Telegraph*, April 14, 1875, p. 4.

"Early in the month": "Travelling in Italy," *London Evening Standard*, August 1, 1893, p. 3. (The source refers to Italy's currency as "francs," though this was the common term for lira in many parts of the country.)

Speed Racer: "Jackrabbit shows auto racers how to run," *Alton Evening Telegraph*, January 10, 1933, p. 2.

a gift to her from some of the students in 1936: "Sniffy is dead; famed rabbit dies of old age," *Calexico Chronicle*, January 27, 1944, p. 1.

staying in fancy hotel rooms: "Globe trotting rabbit," *PIX*, August 19, 1939, p. 46.

Leo had pitched Sniffy: "Sniffy, trained rabbit, to appear on radio," *Calexico Chronicle*, March 9, 1939, p. 1.

"the world's most widely-traveled rabbit": "Leo Watts says Calexico rabbit 'stole' air show," *Calexico Chronicle*, April 7, 1939, p. 1.

fan of the carrots and lettuce: "Leo Watts says Calexico rabbit 'stole' air show," *Calexico Chronicle*, April 7, 1939, p. 1.

They then made their way to Washington, DC: "20,000 children with eggs trample White House lawn," *The Evening Star*, April 10, 1939, p. A-3.

The well-traveled rabbit died in her sleep: "Sniffy is dead; famed rabbit dies of old age," *Calexico Chronicle*, January 27, 1944, p. 1.

"I like anything furry": Interview with Helen Parriss, February 12, 2020.

"She is wild": "Immigrant Spot finds a home," *Norfolk North News*, October 30, 2003, p. 10.

"She went on to live": Email from Wendy Valentine, February 5, 2020.

Chapter Eight: Bunny Biology

In the twilight and the night: Henry David Thoreau, *Walden* (Longmans, Green, and Co., 1910), p. 222.

binocular zone of approximately 24 percent: "Visual Depth Perception in the Animal Kingdom," from *Perceiving in Depth, Volume 3: Other Mechanisms of Depth Perception*, edited by Ian P. Howard (Oxford University Press, 2012), p. 255.

Rabbits compensate: Susan E. Davis and Margo DeMello, *Stories Rabbits Tell: A Natural and Cultural History of a Misunderstood Creature* (Lantern, 2003), p. 15.

"I particularly like the way": Email from Dr. David L. Williams, April 8, 2020.

96–49,000 Hertz: Henry Heffner and Bruce Masterton, "Hearing in Glires: Domestic rabbit, cotton rat, feral house mouse, and kangaroo rat," *The Journal of the Acoustical Society of America*, Volume 68, Issue 6, December 1980.

Endnotes

360–42,000 Hertz: https://www.lsu.edu/deafness/HearingRange.html

not even in the top ten: https://www.hiddenhearing.co.uk/blog/2018/the-top-10-animals-with-the-best-hearing

rabbits eavesdrop: Email from Shaina Rogstad, PhD candidate in geosciences at the University of Massachusetts Amherst, June 16, 2020. Shaina described watching an Eastern cottontail clearly listening and responding to the calls of birds and squirrels in her backyard.

100 million olfactory receptors: Lloyd M. Beidler, "Gustatory and Olfactory Receptor Stimulation," from *Sensory Communication*, edited by Walter A. Rosenblith (Cambridge, Mass., MIT Press: 1961), p. 151.

a dog's nose has between: Alexandra Horowitz, *Being a Dog: Following the Dog Into a World of Smell* (Scribner, 2016), p. 148.

A Very Long Life: https://www.guinnessworldrecords.com/world-records/70887-oldest-rabbit-ever

rabbits have about 17,000 taste buds: Diane Ackerman, *A Natural History of the Senses* (Vintage Books, 1995), p. 138.

As the food travels from the mouth: I am grateful to Dr. Cherie Connolly, medical director of the Compass Veterinary Clinic in Lake Oswego, Oregon, for explaining to me the intricacies of rabbit digestion.

researchers based in Sweden, Spain, and Portugal: Irene Brusini, et al., "Changes in brain architecture are consistent with altered fear processing in domestic rabbits," *Proceedings of the National Academy of Sciences of the United States of America*, Volume 115, June 2018.

a breathtaking 3,745,584 offspring in four years: https://rabbit.org/how-many-rabbits-can-a-rabbit-make/

maybe with help from the father: R. M. Lockley, "Social structure and stress in the rabbit warren," *Journal of Animal Ecology*, Volume 30, Number 2, November 1961, p. 408.

functionally deaf and blind at birth: Benôist Schaal, Gérard

Coureaud, et al., "Many Common Odour Cues and (at Least) One Pheromone Shaping the Behaviour of Young Rabbits," from *Lagomorph Biology: Evolution, Ecology, and Conservation*, edited by Paulo C. Alves, Nuno Ferrand, and Klaus Hackländer (Springer, 2008), p. 190.

rabbits can smell the protective amniotic fluid: Benôist Schaal, Gérard Coureaud, et al., "Many Common Odour Cues and (at Least) One Pheromone Shaping the Behaviour of Young Rabbits," from *Lagomorph Biology: Evolution, Ecology, and Conservation*, edited by Paulo C. Alves, Nuno Ferrand, and Klaus Hackländer (Springer, 2008), p. 191.

a mammary pheromone: Gérard Coureaud, Rachel Charra, et al., "A pheromone to behave, a pheromone to learn: the rabbit mammary pheromone," *Journal of Comparative Physiology*, Volume 196, October 2010, pp. 779–90.

consuming some of the hard fecal pellets: Benôist Schaal, Gérard Coureaud, et al., "Many Common Odour Cues and (at Least) One Pheromone Shaping the Behaviour of Young Rabbits," from *Lagomorph Biology: Evolution, Ecology, and Conservation*, edited by Paulo C. Alves, Nuno Ferrand, and Klaus Hackländer (Springer, 2008), pp. 192–3.

begin eating nest material: Benôist Schaal, Gérard Coureaud, et al., "Many Common Odour Cues and (at Least) One Pheromone Shaping the Behaviour of Young Rabbits," from *Lagomorph Biology: Evolution, Ecology, and Conservation*, edited by Paulo C. Alves, Nuno Ferrand, and Klaus Hackländer (Springer, 2008), p. 190.

rabbits and hares tend to be paler: Susan Lumpkin and John Seidensticker, *Rabbits: The Animal Answer Guide* (Johns Hopkins University Press, 2011), p. 50.

7 to 8 percent of the rabbit's body weight: Katherine Quesenberry and James W. Carpenter, *Ferrets, Rabbits and Rodents: Clinical Medicine and Surgery*, Third Edition (Elsevier Saunders, 2012), p. 161.

biologist Rachel Simons describes: Email from Rachel Simons, January 17, 2020. (In a 1961 journal article describing his study of rabbits, Ronald Lockley referred to their locomotion as a "stiff-legged gait." See R. M. Lockley, "Social structure and stress in the rabbit warren," *Journal of Animal Ecology*, Volume 30, Number 2, November 1961, p. 394.)

"The rest of the rabbit's body": Susan E. Davis and Margo DeMello, *Stories Rabbits Tell: A Natural and Cultural History of a Misunderstood Creature* (Lantern, 2003), p. 22.

sprint at 30 miles an hour: Email from Rachel Simons, January 17, 2020.

"I came up with the idea": Email from Dirk Semmann, July 8, 2019.

Chapter Nine: Rabbits in the Home

House rabbits are not a fad: Marinell Harriman, *House Rabbit Handbook: How to Live with an Urban Rabbit*, 4th Edition (Drollery Press, 2005), p. 4.

"For both children and adults": Katherine C. Grier, *Pets in America: A History* (University of North Carolina Press, 2006), p. 12.

especially encouraged for boys: Keridiana Chez, "Wanted Dead or Alive: Rabbits in Victorian Children's Literature," from *Animals and Their Children in Victorian Culture*, edited by Brenda Ayres and Sarah E. Maier (Routledge, 2020), pp. 33–4.

warns her nephew: Mary S. Claude, *Natural History in Stories for Little Children* (Addy and Co., 1854), pp. 47–9.

"Many magnificent specimens": "South London fancy rabbit club," *The Era*, July 30, 1848, p. 6.

"So, there may be pleasure": Mary Allen Hood, "Guard that furniture!" *The Evening Star*, March 25, 1940, p. B-9.

"Herman entranced our whole household": Ron Grossman, "The rabbit habit," *Chicago Tribune*, March 26, 1991, p. 48.

In the same year that HRS was launched: Preston Filbert, "Run on rabbits," *St. Joseph Gazette,* June 9, 1988, p. 15.

Beguiling Bunnies: Email from Marinell Harriman, July 19, 2020.

"an affectionate companion": *Beatrix Potter's Peter Rabbit: A Children's Classic at 100,* edited by Margaret Mackey (Scarecrow Press, Inc., 2002), p. 136.

"inclined to attack strangers": Letter from Beatrix Potter to Mrs. M. C. Grimston, February 12, 1938. See Judy Taylor, *Beatrix Potter's Letters* (Frederick Warne, 1989).

"Benjamin once fell into an Aquarium": Linda Lear, *Beatrix Potter: A Life in Nature* (St. Martin's Griffin, 2007), p. 183.

His cousin Harriett Hesketh noted: Thomas Wright, *The Life of William Cowper* (Haskell House Publishers Ltd., 1892), p. 218.

"Epitaph on a Hare": William Cowper, *The Poetical Works of William Cowper, Volume 2* (William Pickering, 1830), p. 300.

"washing him from head to foot": Cecil S. Webb, *A Hare About the House* (Hutchinson & Co., 1955), p. 28.

"To get him really excited": Cecil S. Webb, *A Hare About the House* (Hutchinson & Co., 1955), p. 50.

"In contrast to this": Cecil S. Webb, *A Hare About the House* (Hutchinson & Co., 1955), p. 32.

three million rabbits kept as pets: Email from Anne Martin, executive director of the House Rabbit Society, March 10, 2020.

140 million fishes: https://www.fishkeepingworld.com/8-reasons-to-keep-fish/

the opposite is true for rabbits: *APPA National Pet Owners Survey 2019–2020,* p. 451.

Rabbit guardians are also more likely: *APPA National Pet Owners Survey 2019–2020,* p. 490.

The Tartes take the baby bunny home: Bob Tarte, *Enslaved by Ducks: How One Man Went from Head of the Household to Bottom of the Pecking Order* (Algonquin Books, 2004), pp. 15–21.

"If we hesitated to say that Hohepa was in love": Jeffrey Moussaieff Masson, *Raising the Peaceable Kingdom: What Animals Can Teach Us About the Social Origins of Tolerance and Friendship* (Ballantine Books, 2005), p. 127.

"I never imagined that a rabbit could maintain": Lisa Ivers, "A Rabbit for All Seasons," from *Touched by a Rabbit: A Treasury of Stories About Rabbits and Their People,* edited by Lucile Moore and Kathy Smith (Infinity Publishing, 2012), p. 11.

Gus, for example, had been adopted twice: Joe Marcom, "Bunny Man," from *Touched by a Rabbit: A Treasury of Stories About Rabbits and Their People,* edited by Lucile Moore and Kathy Smith (Infinity Publishing, 2012), pp. 28–9.

"Our bunnies continue to reveal": Marinell Harriman, *House Rabbit Handbook: How to Live with an Urban Rabbit,* 4th Edition (Drollery Press, 2005), p. 4.

Ethologist Konrad Lorenz has suggested: Konrad Lorenz, "The innate forms of potential experience," *Zeitschrift für Tierpsychologie,* Volume 5, 1943, pp. 233–519.

they have been bred to look "cute": Jade C. Johnson and Charlotte C. Burn, "Lop-eared rabbits have more aural and dental problems than erect-eared rabbits: a rescue population study," *Veterinary Record,* Volume 185, Issue 24, December 2019.

Ronald Lockley put it best: R. M. Lockley, *The Private Life of the Rabbit* (Andre Deutsch Limited, 1964), p. 144.

Acknowledgements

Although I have years of firsthand experience with domesticated rabbits, I could not have accomplished what I set out to do with this book without the assistance of archeologists, researchers, biologists, scholars, and other experts in multiple countries, and I am indebted to them for their patience. In particular, my thanks to members of the UK's Easter E.g. team: Dr. Carly Ameen, Dr. Thomas Fowler, Prof. Greger Larson, Dr. Luke John Murphy, Dr. Philip A. Shaw, and Prof. Naomi Sykes, all of whom took the time to speak with me about their work.

I am also grateful to Dr. Cherie Connolly, medical director of the Compass Veterinary Clinic in Lake Oswego, Oregon, for explaining to me the intricacies of rabbit digestion; to Dr. Rachel Simons of the University of Southern Maine for describing the biomechanics of rabbit locomotion; to Dr. David Williams, author of *Ophthalmology of Exotic Pets* and an instructor of veterinary ophthalmology at the University of Cambridge, for helping me understand rabbit vision; and to Dr. Jin Meng, a paleontologist at the American Museum of Natural History, for guiding me through the rabbit's evolutionary timeline.

My thanks to Dr. Joanna Meacock, curator for British Art at Glasgow Museums, who helped me appreciate the deeper significance of Henry Raeburn's painting *Boy and Rabbit*; as well as to Dr. Christof Metzger, Dürer specialist and chief curator at the Albertina Museum in Vienna; to Béatrice de Chancel-Bardelot, curator in charge of the tapestries at Musée de Cluny; to Dr. Christopher de Hamel, expert on medieval manuscripts; and to art historian Sue Andrew. Thank you to Libby Joy of the Beatrix Potter Society and to Brenda Davies of the Royal Society of British Artists. Speaking of artists, Sam Cannon, Karla Sachse, and Hunt Slonem were all extremely generous with their time.

Thanks to Dr. John Baker, associate professor in name

studies at the University of Nottingham, for his guidance on rabbit-themed locations; to Dr. Polina Perelman of Russia's Institute of Molecular and Cellular Biology for information about rabbit DNA; to Dr. Dirk Semmann for his insights about rabbit behavior; to linguistic scholar Dr. Anatoly Liberman; to folklore experts Prof. Martha Bayless and Prof. Ronald Hutton; and to Dr. Robert Symmons, curator of the Fishbourne Roman Palace and Gardens.

I confess I was conflicted about including Bugs Bunny in this book, and I am very grateful to Dr. Christopher Lehman, professor of ethnic studies at St. Cloud State University, and Dr. Nicholas Sammond, professor of Cinema and Media Studies at the University of Toronto, for their insights on how this character fits into the history of racism in animation.

Additional gratitude goes to Marcy Berman, Anne Martin, Wendy Valentine, Helen Parriss, Margo DeMello, Keridiana Chez, Barbara J. King, Marinell Harriman, Kim Stallwood, Jonathan Barrett, Tom Ryan, Lisa Stein, and Saliann St-Clair, who each offered guidance, encouragement, or important details.

Special thanks to Tara Baxter and Heidi Margocsy.

Of course, *The Way of the Rabbit* would not exist at all were it not for Tim Ward of Changemakers Books and the many talented people there, including my meticulous editor Mollie Barker, cover designer Nick Welch, text designer Stuart Davies, production manager Andrew Wells, and print manager Mary Flatt.

My abiding thanks and love to my wife, Lauren, for her never-ending patience and support as the months I spent talking about rabbits and their history became years, and those years of discussion gradually became this book. I don't know what I would do without you.

Finally, my heartfelt gratitude to the world's countless rabbit advocates, who work tirelessly to rescue and rehome these gentle animals, raise awareness about the many ways they are exploited, and conserve their populations as human activities threaten their habitats.

Index

About the Author

Mark Hawthorne has fostered numerous house rabbits, including seven he adopted. He has caught and rescued abandoned rabbits, volunteered with rabbit rescue groups, and educated people about rabbits through his published writing and public outreach. His other books include *Striking at the Roots: A Practical Guide to Animal Activism*, *Bleating Hearts: The Hidden World of Animal Suffering*, and *A Vegan Ethic: Embracing a Life of Compassion Toward All* (all published by Changemakers Books). He and his wife, Lauren, live in Northern California. You can read more of Mark's writing at MarkHawthorne.com.

Outside the Vienna State Opera with Ottmar Hörl's sculpture of a pink hare, the artist's homage to *Young Hare* by Albrecht Dürer. Photo by Lauren Ornelas.

CHANGEMAKERS
BOOKS

TRANSFORMATION

Transform your life, transform your world - Changemakers
Books publishes for individuals committed to transforming their
lives and transforming the world. Our readers seek to become
positive, powerful agents of change. Changemakers Books
inform, inspire, and provide practical wisdom and skills to
empower us to write the next chapter of humanity's future.
If you have enjoyed this book, why not tell other readers by
posting a review on your preferred book site.

Recent bestsellers from Changemakers Books are:

Integration
The Power of Being Co-Active in Work and Life
Ann Betz, Karen Kimsey-House

Integration examines how we came to be polarized in our dealing with self and other, and what we can do to move from an either/or state to a more effective and fulfilling way of being.
Paperback: 978-1-78279-865-1 ebook: 978-1-78279-866-8

Bleating Hearts
The Hidden World of Animal Suffering
Mark Hawthorne

An investigation of how animals are exploited for entertainment, apparel, research, military weapons, sport, art, religion, food, and more.
Paperback: 978-1-78099-851-0 ebook: 978-1-78099-850-3

Lead Yourself First!
Indispensable Lessons in Business and in Life
Michelle Ray

Are you ready to become the leader of your own life? Apply simple, powerful strategies to take charge of yourself, your career, your destiny.
Paperback: 978-1-78279-703-6 ebook: 978-1-78279-702-9

Burnout to Brilliance
Strategies for Sustainable Success
Jayne Morris

Routinely running on reserves? This book helps you transform your life from burnout to brilliance with strategies for sustainable success.
Paperback: 978-1-78279-439-4 ebook: 978-1-78279-438-7

Goddess Calling
Inspirational Messages & Meditations of Sacred Feminine
Liberation Thealogy
Rev. Dr. Karen Tate
A book of messages and meditations using Goddess archetypes
and mythologies, aimed at educating and inspiring those with
the desire to incorporate a feminine face of God into their
spirituality.
Paperback: 978-1-78279-442-4 ebook: 978-1-78279-441-7

The Master Communicator's Handbook
Teresa Erickson, Tim Ward
Discover how to have the most communicative impact in this
guide by professional communicators with over 30 years of
experience advising leaders of global organizations.
Paperback: 978-1-78535-153-2 ebook: 978-1-78535-154-9

Meditation in the Wild
Buddhism's Origin in the Heart of Nature
Charles S. Fisher Ph.D.
A history of Raw Nature as the Buddha's first teacher, inspiring
some followers to retreat there in search of truth.
Paperback: 978-1-78099-692-9 ebook: 978-1-78099-691-2

Ripening Time
Inside Stories for Aging with Grace
Sherry Ruth Anderson
Ripening Time gives us an indispensable guidebook for growing
into the deep places of wisdom as we age.
Paperback: 978-1-78099-963-0 ebook: 978-1-78099-962-3

Striking at the Roots
A Practical Guide to Animal Activism
Mark Hawthorne
A manual for successful animal activism from an author with
first-hand experience speaking out on behalf of animals.
Paperback: 978-1-84694-091-0 ebook: 978-1-84694-653-0

Readers of ebooks can buy or view any of these bestsellers by
clicking on the live link in the title. Most titles are published
in paperback and as an ebook. Paperbacks are available in
traditional bookshops. Both print and ebook formats are available
online.

Find more titles and sign up to our readers' newsletter at
http://www.johnhuntpublishing.com/transformation
Follow us on Facebook at
https://www.facebook.com/Changemakersbooks